The Last Piece of England

'The Last Piece of England' was first published in
Great Britain as a hardback, 'Island First Edition',
by Halsgrove in 2002

This amended edition is published as a paperback
in Great Britain by IslandRace.com in 2008

ISBN 978 0 9560111 0 7

IslandRace.com
Lantallack Coach House
Lantallack Cross
Saltash, Cornwall PL12 5AE

Tel: 0845 003 7155
email: richard.barber@btinternet.com
website: www.islandrace.com

Printed and bound by
Rowe The Printers, Hayle, Cornwall

The Last Piece of England

The Story of a Private Island

by

RICHARD BARBER

Island Race.com

Under the eye of The Commodore

Contents

For James, Polly, Rosie and Harriet

INTRODUCTION

Land's End is the most westerly tip of mainland England – at the very end of the Cornish peninsula. Thirty miles beyond Land's End, the Isles of Scilly lie in the Western Approaches of the English Channel; the last piece of England before America.

Scilly is an extraordinary archipelago that was once the peaks of hills. That was before the sea rose to cover the legendary land of Lyonesse that lay between Scilly and Cornwall.

Scilly is a beautiful, magical group of islands that tug at the heart of everyone who visits. Myth and legend hang in the air – from the Bronze Age ritual landscape in the North End to the ruins of St Nicholas Priory in the Abbey Garden in the south of the island.

Many believe that King Arthur and the last of his knights found eternal rest on Scilly – Lancelot, Tristram, Banyan, Bor, Ector, Caradoc and Percival. They were the only survivors of the Chivalry of Britain after Mordred had slain Arthur.

This noble band was pursued by the vengeful Mordred and his army across Cornwall and onto the plains of Lyonesse. They fled west to the hills of Cassiteris. It was then that Merlin, the Great Enchanter, confronted Mordred; raising his arm, the wizard caused the earth to tremble and then to sink below the level of the ocean. With a ghastly roar, the sea rushed onto the plain engulfing Mordred and his army in a boiling maelstrom of foam and waves.

On the hills of Cassiteris, later known as Scilly, the small band of Knights of the Round Table dismounted, knelt on the turf and thanked God for their deliverance. They were safe on what was now an island – separated from the mainland by 30 miles of turbulent sea. The land of Lyonesse that once lay between them and Cornwall had vanished together with all its churches, villages and pastures.

That is one of the old legends of Lyonesse.

Later, the monks of the great Abbey at Glastonbury in Somerset claimed to have found King Arthur's tomb in their grounds, but others prefer to believe that his body was brought to Scilly – the magical islands of the west – to be buried there. Certainly, two uninhabited islands in Scilly have carried his name for centuries....

In the 1,500 years from Arthur's time to the present much has happened on Scilly, but little has changed the timeless beauty of these gentle islands. Two millennia before Arthur was born, Bronze Age people already considered what we call Scilly to be a sacred spot. Many of their religious structures are still there for us to see – a ritual landscape that was ancient even to Arthur and his knights.

In 1991 I came to live and work on Tresco, one of the five inhabited islands of Scilly.

What follows is a compilation of stories, some of which I wrote for the *Tresco Times*. To these have been added unpublished archive photographs and tales passed on by islanders or found in faded newspaper cuttings.

This book is a scoop from the surface of a deep pool. It is not a definitive community history, rather a cherry-picking of island events; it is a microcosm of the history of England that describes an Island Race with all the independence of spirit, stubborn courage and eccentricity that is the bedrock of Englishness.

It's about the Last Piece of England.

RICHARD BARBER

Tresco

The First Chapter
*In which we arrive on Tresco,
meet an islander and walk
into a Bronze Age landscape*

Tresco is a private island, roughly two miles long by one mile wide. It has about 130 permanent residents and, since the 1830s, has been leased from the Duchy of Cornwall by the Dorrien Smith family.

Tresco Abbey

hen I first met Robert Dorrien Smith it was the mid-1970s. A few years earlier he had inherited Tresco while still at university. The island was short of money and together we put together a rescue package based on timesharing some of the holiday cottages on 40-year agreements.

'Stay and help me put the plan into action,' he said.

'Not me,' I replied with the brashness of one who had just turned thirty, 'I'm not going to live on some remote island, I am off to make my fortune in the big wide world....'

Seventeen years later, older and wiser, I returned to Tresco with my artist wife Kathy to manage Tresco's holiday cottages.

On a November day in 1991 we arrived in Penzance in the far west of Cornwall. We dropped off the hire car and took a taxi to the heliport, a low, single-story building, with a hangar and a grass field separated from the main road by a wooden fence. The place had a friendly rural feel; the staff smiled and had healthy tans; the passengers seeming grey by comparison, after their long drive almost to the end of Cornwall.

The helicopter seated nearly 30 people and every seat was taken as we lifted off from the grass field in a gentle, stepped ascent.

Arriving on Tresco

Below, the roof of a supermarket glinted in the sun, and soon we could see the mass of St Michael's Mount on one side and Penzance on the other. We flew west over the Cornish peninsula towards Land's End. At last we relaxed; on our way to a new life on a small island. No longer did we need to own a car, a house – or a mortgage. Life would be simple and uncomplicated.

Below us the patchwork field system of Penwith, the most westerly district in mainland England, was marked by stone 'hedges' laid by early Bronze Age men marking their boundaries – the oldest constructions in continuous use in the world.

The patchwork fields of Penwith

...we took our seats on a covered trailer towed by a tractor

The Longships lighthouse, the final tip of mainland England, passed beneath us and we started out across 30 miles of angry sea.

Five hundred feet below, the Western Approaches were streaked by wind and clumps of brown seaweed ripped from rocks.

Fifteen minutes later we landed on Tresco, settling onto a well-cut field that appeared to double as a cricket ground. Next to us was the Abbey Garden where luxuriant, sub-tropical foliage hinted at all kinds of exotic plants.

Behind the Garden, the granite pile of the baronial Tresco Abbey – a style beloved of Victorians everywhere – commanded the landscape.

We could see the Union flag flying high from the Abbey flag-staff. At one end of the building stood a stone tower. This contained the Tower Flat where we were to be quartered.

We collected our bags from outside the garden-shed structure that was both 'control tower' and 'terminal'.

We took our seats on a covered trailer towed by a tractor. The helicopter and its raucous clatter disappeared back to Penzance, and the total silence of the island descended like a velvet curtain.

It's hard to describe the effect of total silence. Very few people experience it – the mainland noise of neighbours, traffic and aircraft is almost totally pervasive in the 21st century.

We had arrived with the din of the helicopter ringing in our ears, and now all was perfect peace and tranquillity. We sat waiting for the tractor driver. We were on island time. No one was in a rush.

Our driver was one of the fire-crew and so could not be dismissed to drive us until the helicopter was several miles away. After a few minutes we were on our way.

Five minutes later we stood with our bags in the Tower Flat – up a flight of stairs from the courtyard of the Abbey.

Outside, the sun illuminated the brown gorse with golden warmth. Beyond lay the vivid blue of the sea and the distant Eastern Isles. We looked down from the Tower on a view that contained a clarity and variation of colour that neither of us had experienced.

'A drink!' I cried.

The ice cubes crackled as the pale brown malt covered them. We each took a glass and sank into a well-stuffed chair.

Outside, the evening sun faded and a rosy glow touched the cream clouds. The blue of the sky was now a pale Cambridge shade. It seemed too good to be true – as if a Hollywood film director had lit the landscape with an improbable beauty.

The sun had gone when we turned off the light that night. The first stars were visible, bright against the velvet sky. In the silent night we slept the sleep enjoyed by the young, the old and those who have travelled all day. It had been a very long day.

Beyond lay the vivid blue of the sea and the distant Eastern Isles

fter breakfast, we set forth to spend our first day on the island. We were about to meet our first islander.

In the back hall of the Abbey, a couple of big deep-freezes murmured quietly. Various crates were stacked neatly around. Almost hidden behind the open door of a large cupboard a pair of legs encased in gumboots was visible. I waited.

Eventually, the cupboard door swung back and a stocky man in glasses stood up. He observed us without comment. 'Good morning,' I said.

'Morning'. This with only a cursory glance at us.

He busied himself with a long stick cut from a sapling. It was probably about 8 foot long, and he carefully split the top of it with a large penknife. Finally, he finished. Only then did he look at us.

'This should do it,' he said. He took a slice of bread out of his pocket and fixed it into the splice he had made at the top of the stick. He looked at it proudly, and waved it about. It swished like a good fishing-rod, and the bread stayed firmly fixed in the splice.

'Perfect....'

I cannot remember what I thought he might be about to do with his creation. Some kind of arcane Scillonian fishing implement? Perhaps the islanders – when their long day was over – eked out frugal meals with eels caught with long poles and bits of bread. The truth was different and more bizarre.

'Come on,' he said, and shot out of the door with the pole. We followed.

In the gravel courtyard that formed the forecourt of the Abbey, he turned and introduced himself. 'I'm the Abbey odd-job man.'

Without waiting for a response he swooped round the yard, waving the stick high above him, the bread flashing white in the sunshine. All the while he made a strange, high-pitched whistle. Some island men passed the gatehouse, looked at him, rolled their eyes and laughed.

'What exactly are you doing?' Kathy asked him, in a strange voice that suggested she wasn't sure she wanted to know the answer.

'Trying to feed the birds,' he said happily.

'Let's get out of here,' muttered Kathy.

We walked on down the drive. Above us the trees bent to a mild breeze. Although it was early November, it felt warm and autumnal. There was no hint of winter in the air.

At the end of the drive, the channel of water separating Tresco from the neighbouring island of Bryher was a dark blue, reflecting the sky above.

There wasn't a cloud in the sky....

We walked up a concrete road past a small wooden shop with a sign that read 'Tresco Stores'. At the top of a hill we took an inviting, puddled lane between two cottages towards fields.

Some interesting-looking stones stood in profile against the skyline.

The lane took us to a T-junction. To the left, a line of islanders' whitewashed cottages. To the right, the lane was banked high and lush with wild garlic. It curved out of sight, tempting us to follow....

An inviting puddled lane between two cottages....

Some interesting-looking stones stood out in profile against the skyline

Around the curve of the lane we came to a field-gate. The deep green of the field rose up to the bright blue skyline. Leaning on the gate, with the light scent of wild garlic on the air and the sun warm on our backs, we had stepped back several hundred years.

This lane had been there since pre-history. To our left the row of cottages were at least three hundred years old, and the stones on the hill above us had stood for millennia.

The lonely cry of a curlew added to the feeling of remoteness. Nothing from the 20th century intruded.

'According to the map,' I said, opening it up 'these stones have the good circular name of Dial Rocks. Stone circle, maybe?'

We climbed over the gate and walked up the hill. The grass was lush and thick. A herd of inquisitive bullocks looked up from their cropping to stare at us. Near the top of the hill we came to the largest of the stones. All around it the cattle had worn out a circle of dirt in the grass, drawn to it as we were. It had that kind of magnetic pull.

The stone was a peculiar shape, and as we got near we saw that it was three stones – one on top of the other. On it, either the weather or the hand of man had created the mark of a cross.

We had thought this stone to be positioned on top of the hill, but it stood well below the summit.

We stroked its rough granite surface, and looked out at the spectacular view that extended over most of the Isles of Scilly.

The two stone crosses on the church gable ends stood in line like rifle sights

To the east lay the island of St Martin's and beyond that the mysterious Eastern Isles that we had looked down on from the Tower.

To the south lay St Mary's and St Agnes, to the west we could see Samson and Bryher. In the field other stones stood erect. 'Stay a minute,' I said 'Let's just take this all in'.

Exactly due east, the church's Christian orientation pointed up to where we stood. The two stone crosses on the gable ends stood in line like rifle sights.

To our north, behind the hotel, a vast pyramid hill with a stone spine rose from the ground. The landscape felt connected, and we felt part of it.

A vast pyramid hill with a stone spine....

A vast marker stone leads us on

A gateway with a stone post framed the rock-island of Men a Vaur

Another gateway, with a stone post that looked like it might have once been a standing stone or had been recycled from a stone circle, framed the nearby rock-island of Men a Vaur.

Walking to the top of the field we came to a stone wall and clambered over to find ourselves in a completely different environment. We had stepped even further back in time and were about to enter the Bronze Age North End....

The pastureland on the hill and the little valley now lay behind us. We had walked through the gateway of Dial Rocks and entered the magical ritual landscape above – a land of heather, gorse and stones.

We soon came to three huge stones, each weighing several tons, piled precisely on each other.

Three vast stones, each weighing several tons, piled precisely on each other

We followed a line of large stones that lead us away from the massive three-stone cairn.

Cresting a small rise, we came to the edge of the cliff. There, pointing back exactly the way we had come, sat another huge stone.

It was shaped like a huge nesting bird.

It looked like a huge nesting bird

A Bronze Age geometry puzzle

Beyond, the North End stretched away – a glorious multicoloured carpet of green, blue, purple and yellow.

It stretched about half a mile in each direction before cliffs dropped down to the sea. To the west we could see the ruins of King Charles's Castle, but otherwise nothing had been built here for three or four thousand years – yet the hand of Bronze Age Man was visible everywhere....

At first glance the carpet of colour was broken only by random rocks and boulders. Soon, it was possible to pick out the mounds of graves and alignments of stones.

We started our march across the moorland....

The carpet of heather sunk under each step, and we kept our eyes down looking for the next footstep. After a while it was like looking down on a miniature forest, each heather plant like a tree and we felt like giants.

The rocks strewn over the plateau were not always large, most were little more than a couple of feet high. Two shapes of stones appeared repeatedly across this landscape.

One sort was shaved down one side as if to provide a sighting-line, the second was shaped like a triangular pyramid. Other stones had water-gathering basins carved out of them that pointed down stone alignments.

Stones shaped like triangular pyramids

Others shaved as if to provide a sighting-line

9

Some had water-gathering basins carved out of them that pointed down stone alignments

We stomped on through this vast Bronze Age geometry puzzle, alignments everywhere, and we both looked forward to coming back to decipher this enigma that someone had written so large on the plateau.

Finally we reached the end of the island.

Moorland gave way to cliffs. The sea rolled in, big Atlantic breakers smashed on the rocks below.

Curious lines of stones across the landscape

Moorland gave way to cliffs

We found a soft mattress of heather behind a rock and out of the wind. We watched, and listened to the power of it all.

Above, seagulls hung in the breeze, lazily finding a thermal, flicking a feather, dipping a wing and rising upwards effortlessly.

They watched everything, particularly looking for any shoals of fish. Suddenly they became bored, let the wind catch them and were swept off down the island, carried away on the breeze.

The sun was warm and we lay back, squinting at the blue sky, the crash of waves in our ears and absolutely nothing going on in our brains.

This was real relaxation, as we slumbered at the edge of the world.

We slept among many from the Bronze Age who lay there. Next to us a Bronze Age tomb marked the landscape – one of many.

What mysteries lay around us? We drifted off into that wonderful netherworld between wakefulness and sleep.... cradled on the soft moss at the most ancient and unspoilt part of the island.

It was the start of our stay on a magical island, and the beginning of a journey of discovery that would reveal an astonishing history – as well as sweet food for the imagination....

Next to us a Bronze Age tomb marked the landscape

The North End

The Second Chapter
*In which ships are wrecked
and photographed on the
rocks of Scilly*

The Kettle

**There are more shipwrecks on Scilly
than anywhere else in the world –
around 530 have been chronicled, but
the real total is probably nearer 900.**

French fishing boat Gue Leongie

From the middle of the 19th century onwards wrecks on Scilly were photographed by the Gibson family. Many sailors drew their last breath in the sea around Scilly after their vessels fell among the jagged granite rocks.

Traditionally, Scillonians treated shipwrecked sailors as their own, risking their lives on countless occasions to try and save strangers who might be out there among the reefs, crashing seas and howling wind....

Shipwreck!

The Scillonian *hard aground off Scilly*

Horsa

Plympton

Lady Charlotte

Paddle-steamer The Earl of Arran

Shipwreck!

Disorientating fog was often the cause of wrecks. Occasionally smaller boats were lucky and grounded gently before easing off again on the next tide.

Even the *Scillonian* – the islands' passenger ferry – suffered this fate on one occasion.

But for most seamen a shipwreck on Scilly was a desperate and deadly business.

These photographs are reproduced by kind permission of the Gibson family.

Minnehaha

River Lune

King Cadwallonn

Serica

Pasteur

19th-century St Mary's, with the Quay in the background

The Third Chapter
*In which the whole of
Scilly very nearly becomes a
19th-century convict settlement
and a naval dockyard*

**Standing at the gateway of the
English Channel, the Isles of
Scilly's naval history over the
last two centuries is a curious
story of what-might-have-been....**

*This photograph of 1870, taken at the time of the Franco-Prussian War, shows the German fleet sheltering
in St Mary's Roads after a storm. All are sailing ships.*

Scilly sits in a vital and strategic location – and for two centuries the islands featured strongly in government plans for the defence of the realm.

In the 18th century, and at the beginning of the 19th, a serious problem for the Royal Navy was the location of their main naval ports. The Royal Navy could take days, sometimes weeks, to tack their square-rigged sailing ships down Channel from their primary bases in Portsmouth or Chatham against the prevailing sou' westerlies.

By the time they reached the Western Approaches, it might be too late to cut off a Spanish or French fleet coming up from Biscay. On the way, ships could become scattered or wrecked in high winds, and the alternative – keeping them at sea – required constant refreshment of water and victuals.

Old Town, St Mary's, in the 1870s

The Isles of Scilly, conveniently positioned in the Western Approaches, looked an ideal place to base a fleet, positioning them right where they were needed.

In 1776, when Britain went to war against the British rebels in her North American colonies, the Admiralty became painfully aware that they had little or no proper charts of the eastern seaboard of America. In fact, if truth were known, they had very few proper charts of anywhere.

Each year, for every ship that they lost in action they lost nine from running aground. Something had to be done.

Captain James Cook

To deal with the chart problem of the American Revolutionary War, the Lords of the Admiralty commissioned *The Atlantic Neptune* – a secret series of surveys and charts of the American coastline – the first truly accurate mapping of that continent's shores and harbours.

A few years later, it was decided to create a *'Hydrographical Office'* where all available charts and maps could be gathered together under one roof. It would be nothing less than the nation's most valuable intelligence resource.

First they needed a *'Hydrographer to the Navy'*, someone who could set up this major programme, and who had the experience and ability to pull it all together. The first and obvious choice was Captain James Cook who had already discovered and charted more parts of the world than any other man.

However, to their Lordships' dismay, Captain Cook had left on his third and last great expedition to try to discover a northern passage linking the Pacific to the Atlantic – a voyage that would lead to his tragic death in Hawaii three years later.

Unable to contact Cook, their Lordships fell back on their second choice – Alexander Dalrymple.

Islanders in 1860

Alexander Dalrymple

Dalrymple was nearly as famous and remarkable as Cook. He had explored extensively through the southern oceans and was Hydrographer to the mighty East India Company. Even Captain Cook had used many Dalrymple charts on his voyages.

Their Lordships were a demanding group of men. They insisted that Dalrymple prove his suitability for the task of Hydrographer to the Navy by producing a test chart. The area they asked him to chart was the Isles of Scilly. It had already been surveyed by Graham Spence in his remarkable 'Survey of the Scilly Isles' of 1792, and now they asked Dalrymple to show his worth by producing a workable chart based on this earlier survey data. It was, in essence, a drawing test.

Swallowing his pride, Dalrymple did as he was asked and produced the chart. Their Lordships were well satisfied and he was given the job – thus becoming the first Hydrographer to the Navy and the founder of the United Kingdom Hydrographic Office. To this day UKHO still produces 65 per cent of all modern charts in the world. Admiralty charts remain a byword for accuracy and legibility and are a Great British success story.

As the new 19th century dawned their Lordships still toyed with the idea of basing a Home Fleet in Scilly. It all seemed so logical.

In 1802 they decided to do something about it. They called for Dalrymple's chart of Scilly – the one that he had produced as his exam. It was still lodged in Whitehall. They blew the dust off it, spread it out and looked at the problem from above.

It seemed perfectly straightforward – they could build extra breakwaters or moles – the islands themselves to some extent would provide a further natural breakwater – and the fleet could shelter and be watered and victualled before setting out on voyages. Building materials would not be a problem, the islands were made of granite weren't they? So they got out their pencils....

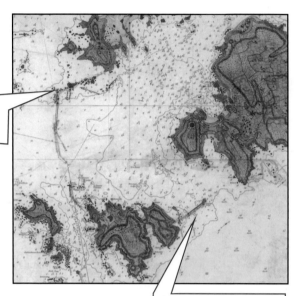

A massive breakwater was drawn from Samson, and then halfway to St Agnes. It was then clumsily rubbed out and re-drawn.

A second breakwater was drawn to close the southern approach to the anchorage.

They called for Dalrymple's chart of Scilly – blew the dust off it, spread it out and looked at the problem from above....

Their Lordships first drew a breakwater from Gugh (part of St Agnes), designed to narrow the channel between St Mary's and St Agnes – one of the main entrances to the anchorage. Any ship approaching from this side would have to pass right under the guns of Star Castle.

A second, even more massive breakwater was drawn from Samson, pointing towards the other side of St Agnes. After some consideration, this was rather clumsily rubbed out and re-drawn.

On paper, scrawled over Dalrymple's immaculate chart, their Lordships had created what looked like a safe sheltered anchorage with breakwaters to add further protection. Guns positioned at Star Castle would provide defensive protection. Now all they needed was to appoint someone to take charge and turn their ideas for Scilly into reality.

The poisoned chalice was passed to Benjamin Tucker, Surveyor General of the Duchy of Cornwall.

One of Graeme Spence's hand-drawn and coloured Views from 1792. This one shows the entrance to Smith Sound. Spence's remarkably accurate work remained the basis of the Admiralty chart for almost 200 years.

THE REPORT

OF

THE SURVEYOR - GENERAL

OF

THE DUCHY OF CORNWALL,

TO

HIS ROYAL HIGHNESS

THE PRINCE OF WALES,

CONCERNING

THE OBSTACLES, FACILITIES, AND EXPENCE,

ATTENDING

THE FORMATION

OF

A SAFE AND CAPACIOUS ROADSTEAD

WITHIN

THE ISLANDS OF SCILLY.

LONDON:

PRINTED BY I. WALTER, PRINTING-HOUSE-SQUARE, BLACKFRIARS;
AND SOLD BY SHERWOOD, NEELY, AND JONES, PATERNOSTER-ROW;
AND J. TRIPHOOK, ST. JAMES'S-STREET.

1810.

This illustration from the report shows the strategic importance of the Isles of Scilly

Benjamin Tucker's Report

In 1810 Benjamin Tucker's report was published – *"The Report of The Surveyor-General of The Duchy of Cornwall to His Royal Highness The Prince of Wales concerning The Obstacles, Facilities and Expence attending The Formation of A Safe and Capacious Roadstead with The Islands of Scilly."*

After a lengthy preamble designed to appeal to the Prince of Wales's vanity, we get to the meat....

First comes an appended report from Humphrey Davy dated 1808 that attests to the satisfactory analysis of drinking water on Scilly. According to Davy the water contained '1/1000 of its weight of saline matter; and one hundred parts of the saline matter containing:

	Parts
Muriate of soda	70
Of Lime and Magnesia	26
Sulphur of Lime	3
Carbonate	1

'The water is not brackish; any subterranean communication with the sea would occasion the presence of a much larger quantity of saline matter, for in that part of the Ocean the salt water contains about 1/32 of saline matter.

'A part of the marine salt which exists in small quantities in the water of Trusco (sic) may possibly be conveyed in the spray of the sea; but there is no reason why it may not be a native impregnation of the spring that feeds the lake.

'I cannot conceive that the water can be improper or unhealthy for common use, or that it can be injured in a voyage.'

With the vital question of the suitability of the drinking water now answered, next came a question-and-answer session designed to establish whether or not Scilly could ever make a safe harbour.

Scillonian pilots pose for the camera sometime in the 19th century

The three most experienced Scillonian pilots were invited to Exeter where they were interrogated. They were described by Mr Tyrwhitt of Scilly as being 'estccmed as the most intelligent and best Pilots for these islands'.

They were Thomas Mortimer with 40 years' experience, James Duff with 25 years' experience, and John Jenkin with 20 years'

experience. Only Mortimer could sign his name, the other two signed with a cross.

Posing the questions were Mr Benjamin Tucker himself, aided by Captain Edward Marsh, Royal Navy, 'commanding the Sea Fencibles upon the islands; and Mr John Johns, Steward of the Islands, and Lieutenant of the Veteran Battalion'.

'It would be a safe and secure anchorage in all winds and weathers.'

Some of the pilots' answers will interest sailors today. For example: which winds occasion the greatest sea and danger, and are most to be guarded against in St Mary's Roadstead?

'From SW to WSW. When the wind gets more to the westward, the water begins to smoothen, as the Nundeeps and Crim break off the Sea; and when the wind is more to the southward, the sea is broken off by Annette, and the Western Rocks'.

'The greatest sea sets from SW, even with the wind at WSW.'

Asked at what time of tide ships in the Roads ride the hardest, the pilots replied: 'With the wind to the westward they ride hardest with the flood; and with the ebb with an easterly wind'.

Tucker had brought with him their Lordships' sketches on the charts and asked the pilots for their views. Carefully he described the proposal so that there could be no mistake.

'Supposing that a breakwater, above the surface at high water spring tides, should be made to the shoal ground south of the Monalter Ledges, from thence towards the rocks called Bristolman's Ledge, as shewn on the Chart; and also a breakwater from the Round Rock to the Spanish Ledge in St Mary's Sound, what effect would they have upon the anchorage, and what degree of safety would be derived therefrom?'

The pilots' answer was precise and suspiciously brief. Without any qualification they apparently answered: 'It would be a safe and secure anchorage in all winds and weathers.'

After answering various innocuous questions, they were then asked 'If the breakwaters in Broad Sound and St Mary's Sound are made, with what wind could ships of the line be carried to sea from the Roadstead?' The answer was once again short and simple: 'With any wind, unless it blew so hard that they could not carry sail'.

John Rennie's suggestions

Next to testify was John Rennie of London. He had never been to Scilly but proposed the construction of a mole in Broad Sound and another in St Mary's Sound to shelter the Roadstead for ships of war. He proposed each mole be 80 feet high, built in the sea where the average depth is 10 fathoms. One would be nearly a mile long running between 'Great Smith and the little Minalto passing over the Scar'. The cost of this would be an incredible £1,690,000 – an astronomical sum for the time.

Rennie continued 'If St Mary's Sound is left open, a great sea would tumble in from the South; and therefore to shelter this Sound and to allow a free entrance for shipping a mole will be required from Gugh island to the eastern edge of the Spanish Ledge a distance of one thousand yards, where the water is, generally speaking four fathoms deep. This mole, I apprehend, will cost at least three hundred and twenty thousand pounds, which being added to the former, makes a total amount of two million and ten thousand pounds'.

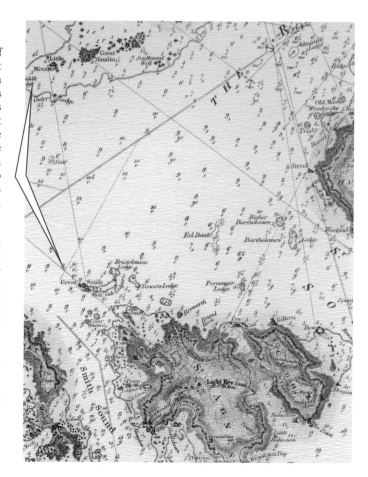

The mole in Broad Sound

Daniel Alexander and James Greig's Survey

The report next included Daniel Alexander and James Greig's *'Survey Proposing Means to form a Roadstead for Men of War in the Islands of Scilly'*. These two gentlemen came down from London pausing only in Exeter to be present at the interrogation of the Scillonian pilots. They brought with them copies of Graeme Spence's 1792 'Survey of the Scilly Isles'.

The splendidly accurate Spence Survey had taken the young Graeme Spence three years to produce, during which time he had been rowed around the islands to make his observations from a gig. The Spence Survey also included the first accurate measurements of the tidal currents.

Alexander and Greig's Survey rejected any idea of building a breakwater out from Samson, or proposals to link Samson to the Minalto rocks, since neither of the constructions would provide sufficient shelter.

The mole in St Mary's Sound

Instead they proposed two breakwaters: one would run from the Scar to Bristol-man's Ledge, providing shelter from prevailing SW and WSW winds while leaving a NW and SW passage for shipping at either end. The second breakwater would join Spanish Ledge to Gugh sheltering the Roadstead from the SE and S gales.

'The Roadstead so formed ... would contain about four-fifths of a square mile, and accommodate about nine sail of the line, with room for getting under weigh in blowing water, and also room to the NE for frigates and ships of less draft of water;

and we take the liberty to add, that in our opinion no other Roadstead can be formed in Scilly.'

But how on earth would this great civil engineering be built? Messrs Alexander and Greig were nothing if not thorough and they produced a detailed plan.

'Before we went to the Islands, we had been informed by masons, etc that the whole Islands were a congeries of uninterrupted granite. We find this not to be so....'

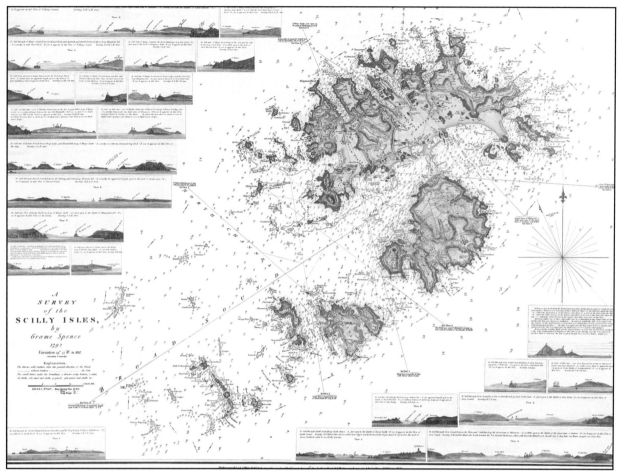

This 1792 chart of the Isles of Scilly was completed by Graeme Spence who spent two years being rowed around the islands in a gig as he carried out his survey and observed tidal streams by following the progress of bottles he had thrown in the sea. The Views he drew coincided with lines of sight on the chart. It was an accurate masterpiece that remained the basis of the modern Admiralty chart for almost 200 years.

Alexander and Greig's detailed proposals would have changed Scilly forever...

What Alexander and Greig had discovered was that Scilly consists of outcrops of granite rather than being solid rock. Their original thought that the islands themselves could be quarried and the stone run down to jetties on a railway now seemed impractical.

While they could see many great boulders around the shores of the islands where they had become detached from the soil by storms, Alexander and Greig were uncertain as to how much suitable rock lay underground ready to be quarried. Nonetheless they applied themselves to describing how the breakwaters were to be built.

The breakwaters 'should be formed of rough irregular shaped (quartoze) blocks of various sizes, from a ton to as great a weight as can well be thrown promiscuously overboard, so as in sinking to jam and find their own beds; having a few smaller intermixed at times to fill interstices'. They proposed buoying the area to be filled and described exact proportions as to width, slope etc.

'It would be advisable to sink one weed with the stone, to induce a growth amongst it, as the work proceeds, as also in calm weather to throw in any kind of shellfish. We had hoped that oysters would have lived here, but we find there are none known in Scilly.'

Next, they calculated the amount of stone required: 'a total of four million seven hundred and thirty thousand and forty tons to be procured and thrown overboard.'

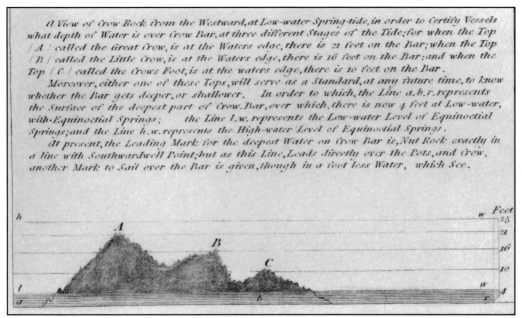

A View of Crow Rock from the Westward, at Low-water Spring-tide, in order to Certify Vessels what depth of Water is over Crow Bar, at three different Stages of the Tide; for when the Top (A) called the Great Crow, is at the Waters edge, there is 21 feet on the Bar; when the Top (B) called the Little Crow, is at the Waters edge, there is 16 feet on the Bar; and when the Top (C) called the Crows Foot, is at the waters edge, there is 10 feet on the Bar.

Moreover, either one of these Tops, will serve as a Standard, at any future time, to know whether the Bar gets deeper, or shallower. In order to which, the Line a.b.r. represents the Surface of the deepest part of Crow Bar, over which, there is now 4 feet at Low-water, with Equinoctial Springs; the Line l.w. represents the Low-water Level of Equinoctial Springs; and the Line h.w. represents the High-water Level of Equinoctial Springs.

At present, the Leading Mark for the deepest Water on Crow Bar is, Nut Rock exactly in a line with Southwardwell Point; but as this Line, Leads directly over the Pots, and Crow, another Mark to Sail over the Bar is given, though in a foot less Water, which See.

Spence was fascinated by the vagaries of the large tides on Scilly. This helpful guide is from his chart

... and created a huge convict settlement

They studied the logbook of Captain Marsh RN for the previous two years, and concluded 'It appears that the winds in the westerly points occupy half the year, and the situation proposed of the work is in the points where this bad weather reigns, and whose effect these works are intended to overcome, so that we do not think it safe to rely upon more than four months, or one hundred and twenty working days in the year.'

They proposed that a special type of boat be designed and built for the purpose of shifting the rock – 'of thirty tons measurement, fifty tons burthen'. They worked out that 200 of these vessels would be required. Each boat would have a crew of three, and at least 1,300 quarrymen would be required – a total workforce of 1,900 men. The cost of the job would be £1.35 million and it would take five years to complete.

Alexander and Greig sign off with the following: 'It behoves us to observe that great difference of opinion may exist in regard to the cost of a ton of stone, so procured, carried off, and thrown down; but in answer, we beg to remark, that the diminution of the cost will depend much on the facilities which may be given by mechanical means; and by a selection of the proper class of workmen to be employed thereupon.

'It has occurred to us, that as the greatest number will be required on shore that considerable advantage might accrue to this particular work, as well as to the kingdom at large, if convicts were employed, intermingling them in gangs with Cornish miners, and with Navigators (a sort of man in the habit of rock and other work relative to inland-canals)....'

Their Report proposed turning Scilly into a convict settlement, where gangs of men would toil at destroying the very islands themselves – dismantling them rock by rock and throwing them into the sea. After five years of this, a naval supply station would be created around an extended Star Castle. Virtually nothing of what we enjoy today would exist.

Alexander and Greig added a Post Script to their Report: 'Before we close the subject, we beg leave to recommend a very obvious improvement of the Tide Harbour of St Mary's that of joining Rat Island with the Main'.

This last point would not be overlooked a few years later when a young man from Hertfordshire called Augustus Smith leased in 1834 the Isles of Scilly from the Duchy of Cornwall.

Meanwhile, their Lordships puzzled over the Report.

Their Lordships ponder the problem ... and do nothing

It was clear that Scilly could in theory be made into a sheltered Roadstead for a Home Fleet, but at a gigantic cost in terms of both money and labour. Could it possibly be worth it?

In the end they did nothing, and as sometimes happens, that was the right decision. Within a few years the problem of where to shelter a sailing fleet would be solved without anyone bringing over any convicts or building a single breakwater.

1n 1805, Lord Nelson defeated the French and Spanish Fleet off the SW coast of Spain finally putting an end to Napoleon's hopes of invading the British Isles. In 1815 he was defeated at Waterloo and banished to St Helena. Their Lordships' main enemy finally died in 1821. Once again the idea of Scilly as a naval base could be put on hold.

However, three years before Waterloo, in 1812, an even more significant event took place in Scotland. A Scots engineer called Henry Bell, inspired by reports of steam-driven river ferries in America, built his steam-powered *Comet* for a ferry service between Glasgow and Greenock on the Clyde.

The Comet

By 1816 the first Channel passenger ferry powered by steam was in operation. The Age of Steam had arrived, and with it came the solution to their Lordships' problem.

By 1834, there seemed little likelihood that Scilly would be needed as a basc for sailing ships since the Royal Navy would, in future, be changing to steamships. With no definite prospect of seeing Scilly being used for a mighty naval base, the Duchy of Cornwall offered the lease of Scilly to suitable applicants.

Mackerel fishing fleet in St Mary's harbour in 1875

In 1835, the lease of the Isles of Scilly was taken up by a charismatic young man from Hertfordshire – Augustus Smith

The lease of the Isles of Scilly was taken up by a charismatic young man from Hertfordshire – Augustus Smith who was heir to a banking fortune with a head full of the utilitarian principles of Jeremy Bentham.

He became Scilly's most enduring influence – the Lord Proprietor who would change everything. Instead of a convict island, and a naval base built with stones torn from the islands, he envisaged a Garden of Eden around which would live happy and contented people, gainfully employed and properly educated.

His contemporaries thought he was mad.

Meanwhile the Navy's best brains, and their Lordships themselves, were still arguing as to whether steam really was the future, or whether sail should retain a place as propulsion for warships.

Although Augustus Smith now held the lease on Scilly, the plans for the naval base were still pored over in Whitehall. There were those who had not given up on the idea.

In 1843 Brunel's steamship *SS Great Britain* was launched and finally, just two years later, the Royal Navy committed to the technology of the future by ordering seven steam-powered screw-driven warships. No longer would they have to worry about a sailing fleet taking weeks to tack down Channel to meet the enemy.

HMS Alexandra *in St Mary's Roads. Built in 1877, she still had masts for sails. Although she quickly became obsolete she had a glittering career as one the smartest flagships ever, to the extent that her captain would not fire the guns for fear of spoiling the paintwork.*

For some, the Steam Age was perceived as an irrelevance....

However, for some, the Steam Age was perceived as an irrelevance and their insistence that sail would always be needed meant that the plans for turning Scilly into a naval base were still not thrown away. It was as late as the early 20th century before the idea was finally abandoned.

The Navy's new weapon – the Dreadnought battleship – was unveiled in 1905 and instantly made all other battleships obsolete. Dreadnoughts drew too much water to use Scilly as a base; Admiral Fisher had to look elsewhere for a naval station and settled on Scapa Flow.

Finally, Scilly really was safe. Or was it?

Within a decade Europe was plunged into the Great War, and Man's ingenuity created new technology and new ways of killing people. A key weapon would be the submersible warship – the submarine. To counter it came the airship and the seaplane.

Now, if you were going to place a squadron of seaplanes to attack submarines that were sinking your ships in the Western Approaches, where would you station them?

The Isles of Scilly, of course... and it was Tresco that would be required by the Navy as an important seaplane base.

This time their Lordships did not hesitate for a moment.

St Mary's islanders pose for the camera

The Fourth Chapter

*In which a young idealist
from Hertfordshire becomes
the Proprietor*

Augustus Smith
1804–1872

Proprietor from 1834

**Augustus Smith lived
through an era of new ideas
in social reform, economics
and politics that captured
the imagination of all
Europeans and Americans
of intellect.**

Just 17 years before Augustus Smith was born, the new republic of America was formed after the Revolutionary War of 1776.

The new American Constitution of 1787 and system of government was created by some of the finest intellects in Christendom; and not just Americans. At the end of the 18th century both Edinburgh and Paris – to take just two examples – were hotbeds of radical thought where men gathered to push the boundaries of democratic and social theory.

The Scottish, in particular, were close to the Founding Fathers, and were hugely influential. Freemasonry was often the link between these social theorists whose anxiety was to test ideas that might better Man's state. That masonic symbolism is still engraved for everyone to recognise on today's dollar bills – a pyramid and eye.

The young Augustus Smith inherited estates in Hertfordshire and a fortune from the Smith banking empire. After Harrow and Christ Church, Oxford, he fell under the influence of the theories of social reformer Jeremy Bentham.

Bentham declared that the objective of all conduct and legislation was 'the greatest good for the greatest number'. Bentham was also passionately interested in both prisons and schools. Education would be an area on which Smith, too, would leave his mark.

Initially, Smith tested Bentham's liberal theories of education and employment at his estate in Hertfordshire. It wasn't long before his landowning neighbours took violent exception to what they saw as a reckless assault on the comfortable *status quo*. Soon Smith was looking for somewhere else to put his – and Bentham's – ideas into practice.

This photograph of a young Augustus Smith in the Abbey archives has been embellished with the painting of his sister, the botanic artist Frances Le Marchant

It was evident that Scilly was not going to be developed as a naval base, so Smith leapt at the chance to take a lease for all the islands. His nearest neighbour would now be 30 miles away across some lumpy sea. The hat of Lord Proprietor fitted him perfectly.

Smith embraced freemasonry, after finding little to satisfy him in the established church. In Hertfordshire he had even been publicly denounced from the pulpit for his liberal ideas. As a mason he was plugged into a modern conduit of radical thought.

He set to work on Scilly with a will that was not always appreciated by the anarchic islanders. The islands had fallen on hard times, but Scillonians were used to looking out for themselves. After all, no one else had ever helped them before.

Their established trades were pilotage of sailing ships that put in for restocking, plus a limited amount of fishing and some profitable smuggling from France.

The view to Old Grimsby, Tresco. Hillside Cottage and Blockhouse Cottages in the foreground

Hillside Cottage on Tresco, now known as Smugglers, in 1875

Smith quickly realised, as had their Lordships in the Admiralty, that steam was replacing sail. Fewer ships would now need to put into Scilly when they could steam to a mainland port for victualling.

The pilotage profession was in decline.

Smith read Alexander and Greig's Post-Script to their Report. He joined Rat Island to St Mary's and thus created a quay in order to attract larger ships to a safe and commercial haven.

The benefits were immediate – for pilots, shipwrights, dockers, farmers and small-holders.

Augustus Smith admired the pilots and the boatmen of Scilly; men who were fine seamen and who enjoyed a close camaraderie.

Smith's dictatorial methods reaped benefit. Better housing was built, youngsters were trained for the merchant marine, and a total of more than 60 trades were established.

He never forgot Bentham's emphasis on schooling. Smith established Britain's first compulsory education programme – one penny a week to attend school, two pennies if you didn't.

Smith, meanwhile, had decided against living on the main island of St Mary's among the majority of his tenants.

Augustus Smith

Early photographs of Augustus Smith's Abbey. Later a tower was added.

Smith realised that Tresco offered him valuable privacy.

He decided to build a property suitable for a Lord Proprietor.

On Tresco he started to spend his fortune on building a house and garden that would be the envy of his friends, and would earn him the nickname 'Emperor'.

Like many Victorian bankers and successful merchants he favoured the solid baronial style that could be built easily from the indigenous granite. It was a style that was also popular in the granite Highlands of Scotland.

He called the house Tresco Abbey, since it stood near the remains of the old St Nicholas Priory.

Smith started the Tresco Abbey Garden in the quarry from which he took the great chunks of granite for this baronial pile.

The Garden site was well chosen with plenty of water from a well while the quarry gave excellent protection from the wind. Then,

as now, it enjoys its own micro-climate.

He built walls and planted windbreaks. From around the world came plants brought back by sea captains who had once lived on Scilly, and knew what he wanted. Many of them were

graduates of his compulsory schooling programme.

He established links with Kew Gardens through Sir William Hooker, and traded plants with many of the other great Victorian plant-collectors in Britain and abroad.

Tresco Abbey Garden

Augustus Smith (far right) and friends pose in front of the old Priory arch that is still a feature of the Abbey Garden

Soon Tresco Abbey Garden was famous as a place where – thanks to the Gulf Stream – temperate plants thrived outdoors. Visitors began to come to Tresco. Smith then started a collection of ships' figureheads from local wrecks as an additional attraction. He had put Tresco on the tourist map.

The remains of the old St Nicholas Priory

Gardeners in front of aloes on the Middle Terrace

Augustus Smith

Smith was famous not just for what he did on Tresco....

On a plaque outside Tresco Abbey Garden he had chiselled the message: *'All islanders are welcome to walk in these gardens'.*

The freedom of Britons everywhere to enjoy the nation's open spaces had started to become a crusade for Smith. It would make his name.

Smith not only welcomed visitors to his own grounds, he started to fight tenaciously for the public's right to wander in all open spaces. His most famous campaign, *'The Battle of Berkhamsted Common'*, is a landmark in conservation history.

As Liberal MP for Truro, Augustus Smith distinguished himself by championing the rights of the public against the claims of the Crown and the Duchy of Cornwall to the ownership of the foreshore on the coast.

It is every Briton's birthright to have access to the shoreline, and one that as an island race we now take for granted. It is one of Augustus Smith's lasting achievements that he made sure this right became enshrined in law.

In 1865 Britain's oldest conservation body, The Commons, Open Spaces and Footpaths Society, was created to guarantee every Briton's rights to walk on common land.

It faced its first serious challenge – from Lord Brownlow of Ashridge. His Lordship decided unilaterally to fence off Berkhamsted Common in order to keep the common man out.

He reckoned without Augustus Smith....

Island scenes, 1875

Landing the fish on St Mary's

Picnic at Piper's Hole on Tresco

Augustus Smith

The Battle of Berkhamsted Common

At the age of 62, Augustus Smith took up the cudgel on behalf of The Commons, Open Spaces and Footpaths Society against his former neighbour – a powerful and well-known aristocrat.

Despite his busy political life and deep involvement with his beloved Tresco and the new Garden there, Smith championed the cause of the public's freedom to roam on common land. Once again, a basic right of the British people enshrined since Saxon times was under threat. He was not a man to stand by and let that happen.

Augustus Smith reckoned that if one man could unilaterally fence off common land, then it was reasonable for another unilaterally to un-fence it. He recruited a team of navvies and commissioned two contractors to oversee them. They were to be sent by rail to Tring and then on to Berkhamsted Common to dismantle Lord Brownlow's two miles of park fencing under the cover of darkness.

The two contractors agreed to meet at a pub near Euston Station before catching the train to Tring. They discussed their strategy in much detail over plenty of strong ale, before rolling out of the pub to discover that they had missed the last train.

Meanwhile a team of 120 navvies had arrived at Tring station in the middle of the night without a leader. Fortunately, a legal clerk had been sent down by the solicitor of The Commons Society to observe proceedings. Showing great initiative he cast aside his stiff collar, rolled up his sleeves and took charge of his small army. It was his finest moment.

He marched his men three miles to the Common, split them into working parties of twelve, and gave them tools and instructions.

By daybreak on that March morning in 1866 two miles of fencing had been neatly laid on the ground, and the navvies marched back to Tring to catch the milk train into London.

Four years of a famous legal battle followed before the Berkhamsted Common affair eventually resolved itself in a famous victory for The Commons Society and Augustus Smith.

It became a model and inspiration for all conservation bodies since.

Augustus Smith is justly famous for his incredible Garden at Tresco Abbey, and for creating the dynasty that has continued his work on the island. If one considers the 5,500 years of human occupation on Scilly as one day, then he arrived about three-quarters of an hour before midnight. Yet no other man has left such an indelible mark on Scilly.

He had created an extraordinary and successful community on Scilly. He was not often thanked for it. It was his genius to discover and apply the paradox of feudalism: if one man owns everything, then no one else can own anything. Thus, since no one owns anything an equal and classless society is created that avoids the divisive cancer of consumerism. There are two important provisos; it can only work in a small community, and it relies on trust: that the 'Emperor' is benevolent, and that the employees are loyal.

His experiment is unlikely to be repeated elsewhere in Britain, but it is a measure of its lasting success that every year hundreds of visitors come to Tresco to share for a short while the benefits of a way of life that disappeared long ago on the mainland.

Three years after his victory in the battle of Berkhamsted Common Smith was dead, aged 68. He died in Plymouth on his way back to Tresco. He never forgave the Duchy for their arrogance in the battles that he had with them over access to the foreshore. He therefore refused to be buried on any Duchy land – and that included Tresco – so he was interred in the graveyard at St Buryan in Cornwall where, on a clear day, you can just see Scilly.

Curiously, his hero Jeremy Bentham also held firm ideas about where his body should lie. His clothed skeleton is on public view in University College, London which he founded.

Augustus Smith wearing the regalia of a senior mason

Augustus Smith never married, and never expected that his closest relative – his nephew Thomas – would have the inclination or the means to take the lease.   As a result he bequeathed the agreement back to the Duchy of Cornwall provided they bought it back on his terms.

They refused to accept it....

Augustus Smith admired the pilots of Scilly and enjoyed their company. Here he is photographed with them – sitting at the front holding his hat, the only one not looking at the camera

The Fifth Chapter

*In which a 3,243-ton steel
ship is lost in seconds, and
the men of Bryher perform
a heroic rescue*

**Six months before
Augustus Smith died in
Plymouth, a shipwreck
and rescue took place on
Scilly that remains an
inspiration to all who sail
in these waters.**

ugustus Smith was very close to the pilots of Scilly whom he admired for their character and professionalism. He was on the mainland when this incident happened, and died shortly afterwards.

This is possibly why the story of the *Delaware* never had the publicity that it deserved, and is little known outside Scilly.

The men involved – almost the entire male population of Bryher – put their lives at risk in a heroic attempt to save lives in horrendous conditions a few days before Christmas.

No one ever thanked them, no one ever acknowledged what they had done and no one rewarded them.

This is the extraordinary story of the *Delaware....*

Today, traditional gigs race each other every week in the summer

Looking out towards Mincarlo from Bryher on a calm day around the time of the wreck

She was considered a large vessel for her time – an iron steamship of 3,243 tons, built in 1865, but also rigged for sail. On 18 December 1871, exactly a week before Christmas Day, the *Delaware* left Liverpool bound for Calcutta with a cargo of cotton, silks, sheet lead and tin. She had a crew of 44 men.

The Bryher pilots first caught sight of her two days later on 20 December. A strong nor'westerly gale had grown to storm force. It was savage weather. In the huge streaky Atlantic rollers, now breaking into foam, the pilots could see the *Delaware* fighting for her life off Bryher and being swept towards Hell Bay.

She was being pushed towards the Norrard Rocks and Tearing Ledge. If she hit there, her fate would be sealed.

The Bryher men raced to the summit of South Hill with telescopes to get a better view of the impending disaster. To their distress they could only watch helplessly.

On board the *Delaware* all 44 men fought frantically to save their ship. The engines were red-hot as they tried to force maximum power from the screw. Eventually – and fatally – the engines had to be stopped before they exploded under the pressure.

Now totally without power, the captain ordered a jib-sail to be hoisted in an attempt to guide the ship between Mincarlo and the other rocks.

If he could just get the ship to run before the wind she would avoid the reef and come inside Mincarlo to calmer waters....

To the despair of the crew, and those on the shore, the jib-sail was carried away by the gale within a few minutes.

The remnants of the canvas cracked like a whip in the rigging, as they desperately struggled to raise a stay-sail – their last hope. No sooner was it raised than it, too, was swept away in tattered shreds.

The seas were mountainous – rising up like the sides of houses with foam whipping off their crests in the screaming gale.

Without power, either from her engines or sails, the *Delaware* wallowed broadside-on in the swell, one second in the trough of the waves, the next lurching to the crest, being lifted up like a toy in the bath.

The poor souls on board could now only commit themselves to the Almighty.

The islanders – long hardened to the power of the sea – could not believe what happened next. A huge wave completely enveloped the *Delaware*. The great steel ship disappeared from view under a wall of water.

When she reappeared, horrified onlookers could see that the entire superstructure had been ripped off by the jagged rocks over which she had been rolled. She was now a naked hull. The next sea broke over her – and she disappeared forever. No human eye ever saw her again.

An iron steamship had vanished within a few seconds on the Norrard Rocks before their eyes.

A RESCUE PLAN IS CONTRIVED

The Bryher men quickly calculated that in the unlikely event that anyone had survived, they might be carried on wreckage towards White Island – a small uninhabited island of about two acres, fairly flat, covered by long grass and sea pinks, with a rocky shore and a boulder-strewn beach. It is situated a quarter of a mile west of Samson, the largest uninhabited island of Scilly, to the south of Bryher.

They scanned the boiling white seas through telescopes. To their amazement, survivors were spotted – two men clung to half a lifeboat, two gripped a spar, and a fifth hung onto a piece of jagged wood.

Five men were still alive from the crew of 44 that had set out together from Liverpool just two days earlier. The Bryher men never hesitated – a rescue plan was swiftly contrived which the pilots among them considered feasible. It was a brave and ambitious plan.

They chose the best sea-boat they had – the six-oared pilot gig *Albion* with a beam of 5ft 6in and 30ft long. The plan was to carry the gig for half a mile overland to Rushy Bay where she could be launched with a following wind and sea.

The men raced to the gig shed at Great Par. Six oars were lashed across the gig, twelve men took the weight in the crook of their elbow, with their other hand on the gunwale to steady her. Each one struggled with the pain and the weight, but none complained and none would drop the load while there were still souls out there to be saved.

A modern gig, exactly like the Albion, *puts to sea*

Patrick Trevellick

THE CREW ARE SELECTED

When they reached Rushy Bay, ten men were selected to make the rescue mission. Their ages ranged from 21 to 50. The names of those heroes were:

Patrick Trevellick, William Woodcock, James Jenkins snr, John Jacob Jenkins, Richard Ellis, William Jenkins, Stephen Woodcock, Thomas Bickford, John Webber, Sampson Jenkins.

Their acknowledged leaders were coxswain Patrick Trevellick who took charge of the yoke lines in the gig, and Richard Ellis who was to be dropped on Samson to signal back to Bryher where another crew waited with a sister gig, the *March*.

Modern gig crews race during the milder months – the Bryher men were rowing in freezing December

John Jacob Jenkins

They launched the *Albion* and the crew pulled hard as Trevellick steered out into the stormy seas. Pilot gigs are designed to run before huge seas, but the 1/4 in planks twisted and groaned as they gradually edged towards Samson with every powerful stroke.

They finally made the lee of North Hill on Samson and were able to beach. Some of the crew scrambled ashore and dashed to the summit.

THE SURVIVORS' STRUGGLE FOR LIFE

Through their telescopes they could make out the two men on the half-boat being swept towards the rocks of White Island, a quarter of a mile away. As the half-boat struck the rocks one man jumped into the sea and clung onto rocks.

When the backwash left him high and dry he scrambled onto the grassy shore. The second man who had stayed on the boat was then washed up onto the rocks and was able to follow his crew-mate to safety.

Two survivors on White Island....

John Jenkins Snr

Thomas Bickford

The two men on the spar were cast ashore about 100 yards further out on the point of the island that is normally covered at high tide. They were seen to get onto the rocks, but despite a desperate struggle were swept off, sucked away by the current and drowned.

The fifth man, on the piece of jagged wood, was swept ashore where the two survivors had landed. But he had no strength left to get off the rocky beach, and was also swept away, never to be seen again.

The handful of watchers on the summit could see no other survivors, but were able to see how the two men might be rescued. They would have to row the *Albion* further along the shore of Samson, then carry her – yet again – across a 200-yard isthmus and re-launch her on the other side.

They ran back to their companions. It was decided to carry out the plan, and if they reached White Island, four men would jump out, leaving five men on the sweeps to keep *Albion* in the shelter of the island.

But first they had to row further along Samson, beach *Albion* and carry her over the isthmus. They reached the East Par beach without incident, and then began the Herculean task of again lifting and carrying the 30-ft gig.

A HERCULEAN TASK

Progress was desperately slow as they stumbled over seaweed, sand, rye grass and scrub. The force of the gale whipped sand and spray into their faces and eyes. Eventually they reached the bank at the West Par where they faced their most formidable obstacle. The seaweed-covered boulders and stones gave a treacherous foothold, and the gale all but tore the gig from their grasp.

They unshipped the slings and each man grabbed hold of a thwart. If they dropped her on a jagged stone, a plank might shatter and the life-saving mission would be over. With a supreme effort they made it over the bank and laid her on the beach, holding her down against the wind.

A modern gig

All was now set for the struggle against the freezing wind and sea. They left Richard Ellis on Samson to signal their progress back to Bryher, and then they started their heroic pull to White Island.

They met the full force of the Atlantic, with the gale almost slap 'on the nose'. The gig flexed and creaked, the men strained every tired sinew to keep her moving toward White Island. The *Albion* stood on end as each roller passed under her, but slowly they made progress until they were halfway there in the savage wind and seas.

THEY FINALLY REACH WHITE ISLAND

The second half somehow seemed easier to all of them, and they finally made a landing against a stony brow on White Island. They watched for the best moment and then ran in quickly on the back of a wave. As the sea receded the four men jumped out as arranged, and on the next wave the *Albion* floated off again without damage.

The youngest man aboard – John Jacob Jenkins – was the first to reach the two survivors. What happened next was pure farce....

The two survivors gathered stones and were prepared to throw them to defend themselves against the islanders whom, they had been told, were little better than savages. How wrong they were....

RESCUED, CLOTHED AND COMFORTED

One survivor was without a jacket and in bare feet, the other had no trousers, and both were soaked and freezing. The *Albion* crewmen gave them their own socks, jackets and a blanket.

After reassuring them, they then carefully searched the island for more survivors – without success. Eventually the *Albion* returned to the rocky shore, and after lifting the survivors aboard they started the long pull back to Samson – this time with the wind and sea behind them.

Never acknowledged ... but not forgotten

Back on Samson, Richard Ellis had signalled for the sister gig *March*. That crew then repeated their companions' feat of carrying her to Rushy Bay before launching her for Samson.

The *Albion* reached Samson safely, coming ashore on a wave and being hauled up the beach by the exhausted crew. There they left her, while they struggled across the isthmus with the two survivors. At East Par they found a fern rick where they rested for the first time.

When the *March* finally arrived at East Par on Samson the *Albion* crew took her over and fought their way back to Bryher with the survivors. On Bryher they took them to John Jacob Jenkins' cottage, 'Southward', where they gave them hot drinks and put them to bed.

The two survivors were the First Mate – a black man called MacWhinnie – and the Third Mate who had the same name as many of his rescuers – Jenkins.

The men left on Samson stayed there all night and carried the *Albion* back over the isthmus. Next day every man still left on Bryher helped bring everyone and everything on Samson back to Bryher.

First Mate MacWhinnie – one of two survivors from the Delaware

Neither gig was ever used again for pilotage. The *March* had been built to beat the *Albion* – which she invariably did – and other rival pilots then built the even-faster *Golden Eagle*.

The *Albion* pilots later commissioned the *Czar* – the fastest of all – with an extra oar. The *Albion* was sold to Mr A Watts of St Mary's who used her planking to build a 10-ft sailing dinghy. The *March* was allowed to fall to pieces on Bryher.

NEVER ACKNOWLEDGED, BUT NOT FORGOTTEN

Five days after the rescue it was Christmas Day, but the Bryher men who risked their lives in this extraordinary and heroic rescue were never acknowledged, never thanked nor rewarded in any way by any authority.

But at least on Scilly their selfless bravery is remembered and is still looked upon as a glittering example to all who call themselves seamen. If you sail a boat in Scilly, then look over your shoulder and back into history... and tip your hat to better men than us.

Just five years later another even more terrible shipwreck would take place on Scilly, resulting in appalling loss of life.

This time, though, the world's attention would be focused on the islands and the pilots would receive full recognition for their efforts.

The pictures of pilot gigs that accompany this piece are taken from the Frank Gibson Photographic Collection and are of modern gig races that take place every week during the summer on Scilly.

All the gigs are wooden and are exactly the same as the gigs of 150 years ago. Then the gigs would race each other to an incoming ship – the first one there would pilot the vessel into St Mary's. This is how the pilots and their crews made their living. Today, each island has at least one gig and both male and female crews race for trophies.

Robert Maybee's poem

Shortly after the wreck, Robert Maybee – the Scillonian poet from St Mary's – wrote a poem about the rescue of the survivors from the *Delaware*.

Here are a few verses...

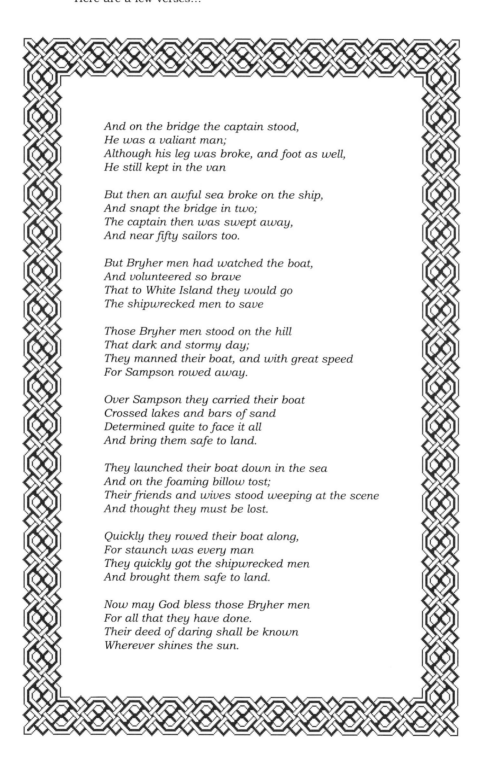

And on the bridge the captain stood,
He was a valiant man;
Although his leg was broke, and foot as well,
He still kept in the van

But then an awful sea broke on the ship,
And snapt the bridge in two;
The captain then was swept away,
And near fifty sailors too.

But Bryher men had watched the boat,
And volunteered so brave
That to White Island they would go
The shipwrecked men to save

Those Bryher men stood on the hill
That dark and stormy day;
They manned their boat, and with great speed
For Sampson rowed away.

Over Sampson they carried their boat
Crossed lakes and bars of sand
Determined quite to face it all
And bring them safe to land.

They launched their boat down in the sea
And on the foaming billow tost;
Their friends and wives stood weeping at the scene
And thought they must be lost.

Quickly they rowed their boat along,
For staunch was every man
They quickly got the shipwrecked men
And brought them safe to land.

Now may God bless those Bryher men
For all that they have done.
Their deed of daring shall be known
Wherever shines the sun.

Old Grimsby

The Sixth Chapter

In which Augustus Smith's nephew inherits the lease of Scilly, creates a cut-flower industry and brings prosperity to the islands

Thomas Algernon Smith Dorrien Smith
1846–1918

Proprietor from 1872

Augustus Smith died unmarried in 1872. His nearest relatives were his brother and his sister.

It was to his brother's son – Thomas Algernon Smith Dorrien Smith – that the lease on Scilly was eventually left.

Augustus Smith's brother, Robert, married Mary Anne Drever, granddaughter and heiress of Thomas Dorrien who came from another family of City bankers and merchants.

In grateful acknowledgement of their second fortune they added the name Dorrien to their surname – becoming Mr and Mrs Smith Dorrien. This prolific couple then produced 15 children. Thomas Algernon, the eldest boy – Augustus's nephew – was a lieutenant in the Tenth Hussars at the time of his uncle's death.

The Duchy refused to accept the lease of Scilly back from Augustus's estate, and so, at 26 years old, Thomas Algernon became the new Lord Proprietor.

In accordance with Augustus Smith's wishes that only a Smith could inherit his estate on Scilly, Thomas Algernon attached a second and final Smith to his surname, thus becoming Thomas Algernon Smith Dorrien Smith.

In 1875 he married Edith Tower, daughter of Augustus Smith's close friend Lady Sophia Tower – without adding any further to his collection of surnames.

This photograph shows Mrs Smith Dorrien (*nee* Drever), seated centre and surrounded by her 15 children and other members of the family in 1902. Her husband Robert had already joined the Great Majority.

Her children, in order, were: Thomas Algernon, Frederick, Theophilus, Walter, Arthur, Horace, Frances, Marian, Amy, Edith, Alma, Mary, Maude, Laura and Dora.

The fecund Mrs Smith Dorrien spent much of her adult life pregnant. Interestingly, only three of her girls married. Perhaps she discouraged them from doing so, since the dowry payments would have removed at least one of her fortunes.

Behind her with the walrus moustache is Thomas Algernon Smith Dorrien Smith, aged 56 and the Lord Proprietor of Scilly. To her right sits Horace Smith Dorrien – one of the very few survivors of the Zulu slaughter at Isandhlwana and Rorke's Drift. Horace later became a general and a hero of the Great War when he refused to retreat (*The Man who Disobeyed*) and held the line against the Germans.

Thomas Algernon was with Baden Powell at Mafeking in 1899. When the Boer siege was lifted after more than seven months, his brother Horace Smith Dorrien was among the relieving troops – as also was Baden Powell's brother.

The elderly lady in front of Mrs Smith Dorrien in the photograph is Augustus Smith's sister, Frances Le Marchant who was well into her nineties by this time.

An up-turn in the islands' prosperity

Cottages in Back Lane, Tresco – now demolished

Thomas Algernon Smith Dorrien Smith arrived on Tresco in 1872 to find that his inheritance – Scilly – had suffered a serious downturn in prosperity.

With no public telegraph system the islands were cut off from the rest of the world; the Steam Age and iron ships had substantially reduced the demand for wooden ships to be built on Scilly. Steam ships preferred the mainland ports like Falmouth, so the pilots' trade had slumped as well. Local fisherman had no easy access to the mainland fish markets, and the market for early potatoes had been undercut by growers in the Channel Islands. Something had to be done.

Thomas Algernon came up with the idea of growing narcissi for the mainland market. Scilly had a

month's climate advantage over the mainland, meaning that the flowers could command a premium price.

By 1886 he was exhibiting 150 different varieties at the St Mary's Flower Show, and had created and organised the trade on Scilly.

St Mary's Quay was enlarged to allow steamers as well as sailing boats from the off-islands to load and unload flowers. It was of value to the fishermen who needed to get their catch to the mainland. He built glass-houses to bring on the flowers even earlier, thus catching the earliest possible market and getting the maximum from the selling season.

In short, he achieved a remarkable turn-around in the islands' prosperity.

PRIVATEERS to BANKERS – The Dorriens

Let us divert for a moment to look at the Dorriens.

John Dorrien, Mary Anne Drever's great-grandfather, had been Chairman of the mighty East India Company in 1760 during the days of Clive. One of his sons then inherited a vast fortune from an uncle – a privateer called Nicholas Magens – that included a mass of silver bullion captured from the French.

It was the largest prize ever taken. In gratitude for his inheritance, John Dorrien's son expanded his surname from Dorrien to Magens Dorrien Magens.

LICENSED PIRATES

Privateering was a profitable business. Privateers were licensed pirates who paid a commission to the Crown and in return had permission to loot and pillage foreign ships on the high seas.

Each king in Europe licensed his own privateers. A certain sort of rogue was attracted to the game, and it wasn't long before privateers found ways to cheat their employers.

AN UPWARD MOBILITY

There was an upward mobility to which privateers aspired. Once they had a goodly stash of gold and silver, they became banks and insurance companies. Many of the country's commercial and financial structures appeared to be run by a 'brotherhood' with its roots in piracy.

To counter cheating by his licensed pirates, the king employed commissioners to watch the coasts and to follow the privateers when they returned. It was not that successful. Particularly when privateers, or former privateers, were appointed in a poacher-turned-gamekeeper philosophy. At least one commissioner was called Dorrien.

CLOUDY CIRCUMSTANCES

The fortune that Magens Dorrien Magens inherited from Nicholas Magens had been acquired under somewhat cloudy circumstances in 1745.

Nicholas Magens had dealings with various French merchants who had commissioned three ships to sail to South America to pillage for gold and silver.

As a privateer, Nicholas Magens sent his own ships to intercept the French on their return and conveniently met them within a few days of sailing into the Atlantic; the fight was brief and the French ships' hulls were miraculously undamaged by English cannon fire.

Landing the fish on Farm Beach after a family fishing trip in 1906

On an island there is always something to do in a boat – particularly in summer and Thomas Algernon enjoyed being on the water. Fishing was a favourite past-time, and the waters teemed with fish – far more so than today, when big 4-mile nets scoop up the entire shoal leaving none to breed and grow.

The captured French crews were mostly uninjured, were well treated and then landed unhurt in Ireland.

Although a massive amount of treasure – in fact, the largest prize ever – reached London safely, complexities involving insurance claims left some people believing that somehow Magens and the French merchants had done rather better out the incident than they should.

However, little of this bothered Magens Dorrien Magens who had inherited the remnants of this huge fortune.

In 1794, the Dorrien family bank *'Dorrien, Rucker, Dorrien and Martin'* changed its name to *'Dorrien, Magens, Mello and Co'.*

MAJOR FINANCIAL DISASTER

Four years later, in 1798, a major financial disaster hit the country, and created one of the most worrying episodes in Britain's history. We were at war with France, threatened with invasion, prices were high, taxation was astronomical and food supplies were low. In addition, there was an acute shortage of coinage. The price of silver was so high that people melted coins down, and gold and copper ones were also scarce.

With no proper means of trading, everyone was badly affected. It was during this crisis, that Gilreay's cartoon showing the Bank of England as a skinny harridan sitting on her treasure chest created the Bank's famous nickname of 'The Old Lady of Threadneedle Street'.

In an attempt to relieve the crisis that this shortage of coinage had created, a group of bankers lead by Magens Dorrien Magens sent a vast amount of silver to the Royal Mint to be turned into shillings. The coins were struck but before they could be distributed Prime Minister William Pitt stopped the process and ordered them to be turned back into ingots. The Government resented being up-staged by a group of bustling City merchants. However, around 20 Dorrien Magens shillings escaped the crucible, were never melted down and are now some of the most sought-after and valuable coins hunted by numismatists.

Eventually, after 18 months, the Government returned the silver. It had been a disastrous venture for the merchants. The shortage of silver for coins lasted for another 18 years, until 1816 when the Prime Minister Lord Liverpool solved the problem by replacing silver with gold and creating a new coin – the sovereign – that stayed in circulation until 1914.

Thomas Algernon with a 16-lb pollock

Sailing was another summer activity, although gentlemen were expected to wear a jacket and tie and ladies a hat, – again rather different to today.

Looking down at the Abbey Garden, with the Abbey and the Eastern Isles in the distance, 1906

Augustus Smith's pride and joy – the Abbey Garden – was beginning to mature and under his nephew's direction it began to rank as a serious botanic experiment of international renown. Plants from South Africa and South America were established, and magnificent Monterey pine and cypress were planted successfully.

The Tower, built at the east end of the Abbey, pictured here in 1906

New Grimsby, 1907

King Edward VII visits Scilly in 1902

The Royal Yacht Victoria and Albert *in St Mary's Roads, 1902*

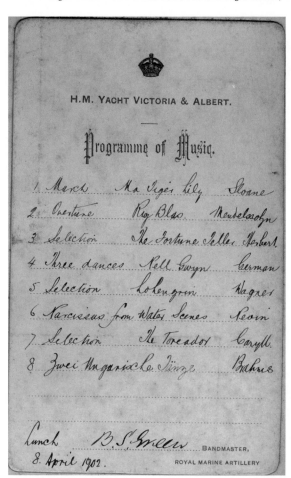

The Programme of Music for the day

The story of how a little Paradise was being created on Tresco had reached the ears of the Royal Family and Queen Victoria visited Scilly in the 1880s.

Later in 1902 Thomas Algernon had the honour of receiving King Edward VII, a year after Victoria's death. The King arrived in the Royal Yacht *Victoria and Albert*, together with a full naval escort.

The guardship HMS Minerva

Thomas Algernon Smith Dorrien Smith

The King embarks at St Mary's

The King with Thomas Algernon on St Mary's and at Pulpit Rock

The grand old Duke of Connaught

Queen Victoria's third son, Prince Arthur, Duke of Connaught, also visited in 1905. The Duke was a distinguished soldier, having been the Commander in Chief in Ireland, and would hold a similar position in the Mediterranean before becoming Governor General of Canada, 1911–16.

He arrived on *HMS Monmouth*, a three-funnelled cruiser that anchored in St Mary's Roads.

The Duke with his entourage, accompanied by Thomas Algernon. **Below:** HMS Monmouth, *seen here off St Mary's, was later sunk with all hands at Coronel by Graf Spee's squadron in the Great War*

New Grimsby from Dial Rocks

Dolphin Town with Old Grimsby beyond. There are virtually no graves in the graveyard and a new road is visible beyond the church. Most of the row of cottages on the left of the road have since been demolished.

Tresco in the early 1900s

New Grimsby Harbour at the end of the 19th century. The New Inn is in the foreground with Dial Rocks cottages on the hill. The left-hand cottage was always left unpainted as a day-mark for shipping.

Palace Row has yet to be built.

By the start of the 20th century a new sheltered field system for growing narcissi was in place and more cottages had been built for workers.

Old Grimsby.   No one can remember what the mysterious obelisk is. By enhancing the picture it looks to be a wood, metal or block construction rather than a natural stone. It has rectangular holes on one side and two protuberances that could be taps.

Thomas Algernon Smith Dorrien Smith

The Abbey Drive

Thomas Algernon and his family of five daughters and two sons lived on Scilly for more than 40 years. He died in 1918, and the inscription on the family monument reads 'He devoted his life unselfishly to these islands and added greatly to their prosperity and beauty'.

The Long Walk in the Abbey Garden, 1907

Family picnic

A family picnic to Bryher. The North End of Tresco in the background

A lifeboat from the Schiller *pulled up on a beach on St Mary's*

The Seventh Chapter
*In which the terrible loss of
the German steamship
Schiller shocks the world.
The kindness of islanders to
the survivors is recognised*

***Thomas Algernon Smith Dorrien Smith
and his new wife returned to Tresco
from a Paris honeymoon in March 1875
and were immediately plunged into a
tragedy that shocked the world.***

***A boatload of cold, bedraggled,
frightened people were found in a
lifeboat in New Grimsby. They had
come from the Schiller, a modern
German transatlantic liner.***

New Grimsby, 1875

Thomas Algernon immediately took charge of operations both on Tresco and on St Mary's....

The story of the *Schiller's* terrible last voyage became headline news around the world. What made it so tragic and heart-rending was that many of those who lost their lives were women and children.

The German Transatlantic Steam Navigation Company of Hamburg was one of the largest shipping lines in existence when they commissioned an iron screw-steamer from Napiers of Glasgow for delivery in August 1873. At 3,421 tons, 380 ft long with a 40-ft beam, the *Schiller* was one of the greatest passenger ships afloat and soon became a popular choice with both German and American passengers.

Shipwreck! *The Schiller*

Embarking in New York

On 27 April 1875 the *Schiller* loaded in New York before starting a scheduled voyage to Plymouth, Cherbourg and her home port of Hamburg.

Before the passengers embarked, a valuable cargo had to be stored in the holds: sewing machines, agricultural implements, flour, feathers for upholstery, kegs of resin and the Royal Mail's bags of letters and packets from New Zealand and Australia.

One very special consignment was delivered under armed guard: 300,000 coins including 20-dollar gold coins worth over £6m in today's money.

With the cargo safely stowed, the *Schiller* received her passengers. There were 120 in steerage-class, 75 in second-class and 59 in first-class. Among the latter was Mr Kornblum, a paper manufacturer from New York who brought with him 85 gold watches, a mass of jewellery and £500 in coin.

Another New Yorker was Louise Holzmeister who looked forward to celebrating her 24th birthday in a few days time. Also on board was champion Cornish wrestler, Richard Williams from Chacewater.

There were 251 passengers and 104 crewmen when the *Schiller* slipped the pier and set sail from New York for Plymouth.

The *Schiller* made excellent time across the Atlantic, and by 7 May was nearing the Isles of Scilly. She was well ahead of schedule.

FOG

At 8 o'clock that evening a thick fog descended. Within 15 minutes, it was impossible to see the length of the ship.

Captain Thomas immediately took in sail and proceeded at 4 knots under power. An hour later, with the Bishop Light not seen or heard, the Captain asked for volunteers from the male passengers to act as extra lookouts. A bottle of Krug champagne was the prize for the first man to see the light or hear the fog bell.

The prize was never collected. At 10 o'clock that night the *Schiller* struck the Retarrier Ledges.

She had managed to pass inside the lighthouse.

COMPLETE PANIC ON BOARD

The engines were put astern and the fatally damaged *Schiller* pulled clear of the reef, but as she wallowed in the swell three huge waves in succession lifted her up and flung her back on the Ledges, this time broadside on.

The dense fog, heavy seas, the darkness, the slippery decks and angle at which she lay combined to magnify the horror of the catastrophe for those on board.

Complete panic broke out among the passengers. Men, women and children rushed to the boats screaming and crying and some of the men drew knives, the better to fight for a place in the lifeboats.

Captain Thomas fired his revolver in the air to restore discipline. Eventually running out of ammunition, he was obliged to draw his sword to drive out the cowardly men from the eight lifeboats.

BOATS SMASHED AND CAPSIZED

Two boats and their occupants were then flattened when the funnel crashed down on them, two others capsized after being cut loose from the painted-up chocks. Another two were smashed against the hull as they were lowered, drowning the occupants.

Just two boats got away safely. On board 320 men, women and children were left to face a night of mounting horror – and a rising tide.

They managed to fire the cannon half a dozen times before the powder got wet and then, hopelessly, rockets were sent up into the blanketing fog.

A GUN IS HEARD...

On nearby St Agnes, the cannon shot was heard but was assumed to be the normal report gun fired by ships as they passed the Bishop. However, a couple of islanders, including pilot Obediah Hicks, wondered....

The gun was also heard on St Mary's and a routine shipping report was sent to the *Schiller's* Agent in Plymouth.

DESPERATION

On board the *Schiller* things were desperate. By midnight she had developed an even heavier list and Captain Thomas ordered all the women and children into the deckhouse structure over the midships saloon.

More than 50 huddled there, weeping mothers clutching bewildered howling children.

At about 2 am, the Captain, the ship's doctor and the Chief Engineer were swept off the bridge by a huge wave that raked the ship from stem to stern. A succession of heavy seas then continued to sweep the ship.

One ripped off the deckhouse roof, the next hurled the occupants into the sea. Men would never forget those screams. All the women and children who sheltered there were drowned.

LASHED TO THE RIGGING

Men started lashing themselves to the rigging, on each of the masts. One iron mast was swept away almost at once, taking all on it under the water.

The other mast stayed upright with men clinging to it. A passenger, Mr Percival, urged them higher before his brains were dashed out by a loose chain just as he reached the Crow's Nest.

Another passenger called West used Percival's body as shelter from the thrashing spray and survived to be picked up later from the sea.

OBEDIAH HICKS WONDERS....

On St Agnes, Obediah Hicks and his crew resolved at first light, 4 am, to take out the gig *O & M* (for Obediah and Mary) into the huge seas and thick fog to investigate stories from other islanders of more than one cannon shot being heard.

They rowed out past Melledgen and Corrigan, and along the length of the Western Rocks, and as the mist cleared for a moment, they saw to their horror a mast and some sails of a large ship protruding from Retarrier Ledges.

The crew of the *O & M* decided to take the difficult passage through the Neck of Crebawathen, shipping several big seas as they pulled desperately on the sweeps to get nearer to the wreck.

They found the sea littered with debris. Above the pounding surf, they heard the dreadful screams of the men in the rigging and those clinging to wreckage.

Then a huge piece of wreckage smashed the rudder of *O & M* and the danger of fatal damage to her ¼-inch planking meant that Obediah Hicks had no option but to order his crew to row for St Mary's to raise the alarm.

Rescue

Obediah was able to pluck five survivors, including Mr West, from the sea before turning away for St Mary's. On the way, they alerted two fishing boats from Sennen that were sheltering from the storm. Both went to the wreck.

THEY RAISE THE ALARM ON ST MARY'S

The *O & M* reached St Mary's at 7 am, and by 8 am the mail-steamer *Lady of the Isles* was steamed up and took both the St Mary's lifeboat and the *O & M* in tow.

The big seas had the steamer's decks completely awash, and eventually the *O & M* had to cut herself free when two of her planks stove in. The gig was lucky to reach land with the crew bailing frantically to stay afloat.

The *Lady of the Isles* found a scene of desolation and horror. The remaining mast by then had fallen, taking those on it to their deaths and nothing could be seen but debris and bodies.

Various small boats continued to scour the seas for survivors and a few were found clinging to rocks. The two lifeboats that got away from the *Schiller* when she first hit the Ledges eventually landed on Tresco with 27 people including the only woman to survive. Of the 355 souls that left New York, just 44 men and one woman survived.

Not a single child was saved.

Lady of the Isles

Preparing a mass grave on St Mary's

Islanders laboured for days to provide a suitable final resting place for the victims

The enormity of the tragedy profoundly affected Scillonians

SADNESS AND HORROR

The vast number of bodies soon presented a problem. Several of the men were recovered stiffened in *rigor mortis* with their fists clenched as if they had fought a last frantic battle for survival.

Many female bodies had to be prised away from the corpses of small children that they were found clutching.

All this sadness and horror profoundly affected the islanders. A large number of drowned children were recovered, many of whom appeared angelic and looked strangely peaceful in death.

Some bodies, on the instructions of relatives, were embalmed for return to America in simple black-painted deal coffins, but the majority were buried in three mass graves in St Mary's churchyard. The granite had to be blasted with dynamite to make room for them.

The islands are plunged into mourning

It was one of the saddest days in the islands' history

Mr Kornblum perished with his watches, as did Louise Holzmeister whose heart-broken husband erected a fine memorial to her in St Mary's church.

Richard Williams, the champion Cornish wrestler, survived and was known as 'Schiller' Williams ever after.

310 souls, mostly German, were dead and the islanders, led by Thomas Algernon Smith Dorrien Smith, plunged into the deepest mourning.

Some bodies were later disinterred for identification by relatives

AFTERMATH...

The tragedy shocked the world. The practice of sounding a gun to report arrival was abandoned at once. Henceforth, it would only ever be used as a distress signal.

Reporters flocked to cover the story. The kindness, compassion and sensitivity of the islanders won universal praise, as did the honesty of poor Cornish and Scillonian fishermen who handed in thousands of pounds-worth of recovered valuables and jewels.

Many bodies were disinterred after burial for identification by their grieving relatives.

Mr Franz Hauser from Iowa hired divers to find the bodies of his two sisters who perished. One was found held firmly in the clutches of a huge cuttle-fish with tentacles over 12 feet long. Mr Hauser died of shock three days later.

The Emperor and Empress of Germany distributed medallions and bibles to islanders, and gold medals to the coastguard and the lifeboat coxswain.

Mrs Smith Dorrien Smith was given a gem-encrusted bracelet with the Empress of Germany's personal thanks for all that the family had done for the survivors.

There is an oddly chivalrous epitaph to the story. Throughout the two World Wars that followed, many believed that the German Navy and Luftwaffe had instructions to spare both the Isles of Scilly and their supply ship, the *Scillonian,* from attack because of kindnesses shown to their countrymen by islanders years before.

Remnants of the wreck

A few remnants of the *Schiller* and her cargo survive to this day. The ship's bridge was recovered, and is installed at the Abbey where it does duty as a foot-bridge to a garden annexe.

Also in the Abbey is a remarkable piece of angle iron that formed part of the ribs of the *Schiller*. Jammed into it by some massive force is one of the gold 20-dollar coins with which the ship had been laden.

At least one sack of letters was recovered and the letters were duly delivered by the Royal Mail. Today those envelopes fetch a tidy sum at auction.

The whole morbid episode remained etched in islanders' minds for generations – partly because so many of the *Schiller* victims were children.

There were also rumours that a large number of the crew and passengers were drunk that night, having just celebrated an officer's 40th birthday.

Later, the Receiver of Wrecks, a mainlander, was strongly suspected of enriching himself from the proceeds of the valuables from the wreck, most of which had been turned in by poor Scillonian fishermen.

Old Grimsby at about the time of the Schiller *tragedy. At least a dozen properties no longer exist.*

The Navy were experts in rigging apparatus for moving guns, and this was sometimes put to use for the amusement of the Dorrien Smiths and their friends

The Eighth Chapter
*In which the islands
enjoy a golden age at
the height of Empire*

The first glorious
decades of the
twentieth century

*Tresco was an idyllic
playground for the Dorrien
Smiths and their friends. It
was the calm before the storm
that would break in 1914.
For the moment, everything
was happiness and light....*

Arthur is the one in the front row studiously not looking at the camera

Squadrons of the Home Fleet fleet lay at anchor in St Mary's Roads off Tresco – symbol of British dominance of the seas.

Thomas Algernon was no doubt delighted to receive a visit from his younger brother Arthur – or to give him his full title Captain Arthur Smith Dorrien, Royal Navy. Arthur was commanding officer of *HMS Rainbow* and would put into Scilly during manocuvres whenever possible.

It was a great boost to the local economy to have the Fleet in, and there was a whirl of social activity at all levels of island society.

The Edwardians on Tresco

Left: HMS Rainbow *was a 2nd class cruiser of the Aeolus class, built in 1891.*

She was not the fastest vessel in the fleet and carried a name that was surprisingly non-aggressive for a warship.

Below: *The Devonport Destroyer Squadron was a different matter...*

The destroyers were rakish vessels capable of very high speed and armed with torpedoes. Their names reflected their lines: Dasher, Sprightly, Falcon....

Above: *The Devonport Destroyer Squadron leave Scilly*
Left: *Firing a torpedo from* HMS Sprightly, *steaming at 20 knots*
Below: *A family party return to Tresco from a visit to the Fleet*

Britannia rules the waves

HMS Revenge

HMS Magnificent

HMS Niobe

HMS Diadem

HMS Majestic

These photographs of the Home Fleet in St Mary's Roads were taken in 1902. The battleships, cruisers and destroyers shown here represent a greater tonnage than the Royal Navy can muster today. Battleships like *Revenge* and *Magnificent*, and old-fashioned cruisers like *Rainbow* represented the old Navy. Everything would change in 1905 when the Dreadnought was launched. In a stroke all but the destroyers would become obsolete.

It also finally removed any possibility of Scilly being needed as a naval base – the water simply wasn't deep enough to float a Dreadnought.

Land of Hope and Glory...

1902 was also the year when the country's second great anthem was played for the first time. It enraptured the Edwardians, summing up their confidence and belief in the national identity and the virtues of an Empire on which the sun never set.

> *Land of Hope and Glory, Mother of the Free,*
> *How shall we extol thee who are born of thee?*
> *Wider still and wider shall thy bounds be set;*
> *God, who made thee mighty, make thee mightier yet...*

But a few years earlier the poet Rudyard Kipling felt the cold shadow of future events and penned his prophetic *'Recessional'* in 1875.

> *Far-called, our navies melt away;*
> *On dune and headland sinks the fire:*
> *Lo, all our pomp of yesterday is*
> *One with Nineveh and Tyre*
> *Judge of the Nations, spare us yet,*
> *Lest we forget, lest we forget...*

1909 – The engagement party of Arthur Algernon and Eleanor Bowlby

Guests from other islands left their boats off Carn Near.

Arthur Algernon, Thomas Algernon's son, later known as 'The Major', was a captain in the Army when he married Eleanor Bowlby.

He had grown up among exotic plants on Tresco and he seized every opportunity for travel that the Army could offer. Apart from anything else it gave him a chance to collect plants from around the world while serving the King.

He served in South Africa between 1899 and 1902 and diligently sent back plants to his father on Tresco. In 1903 he was appointed ADC to the Governor-General of Australia, and helped to set up the Botanic Garden in Melbourne.

Later, while a captain, he joined a scientific expedition to the Auckland and Campbell Islands off the coast of New Zealand.

Celebrations on the Green, next to the Abbey

Arthur and Eleanor surrounded by family

Islanders pose for the camera

Edwardian sport on Scilly

Taking part in sport of all sorts was considered an essential part of being British. It fostered well-being, health and a competitive spirit. The Edwardians soon created a golf course and a tennis court for islanders on St Mary's.

Queuing to enter the Abbey Garden

Enjoying the party

In front of the Abbey 'The Duckery' was home to exotic rhea brought back from New Zealand. They flourished next to domestic fowl, providing just the right animation among the sub-tropical plants.

In the middle of the island a range of greenhouses were built next to the farm buildings. In the picture the men stand next to a large pile of boxes; the start of the export of produce from Tresco to the mainland.

The band plays on...

In 1909 on Tresco, like elsewhere in Europe, the band played on...

No one could foresee the terrible events that would follow in just five years' time. Triggered by an assassin's bullet in the Balkans, a conflagration was started that would claim the cream of a generation.

The Thomas W Lawson *unladen, shortly after her launch*

The Ninth Chapter
In which a sad wreck in 1907 claims the lives of both crew and islanders

The first ever
oil-polluting
wreck of a
tanker

The **Thomas W Lawson** *was the largest fore-and-aft schooner ever built. She was a vessel of radical design and was full to the brim with the Edwardians' latest prize commodity – oil.*

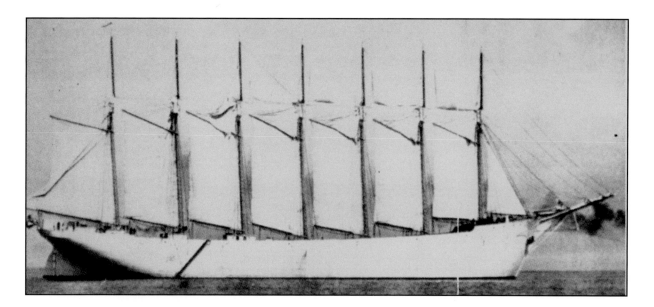

E dwardians were imaginative, confident and excited by the speed of history. They were always ready to push the boundaries of technology.

By the start of the 20th century oil had become a valuable commodity and the need to export it in bulk was essential. This could only be done by ship and soon the first oil-tankers were being constructed.

Sail was still struggling to survive against steam-power. The *Thomas W Lawson* project was a bold and imaginative attempt by the Coastwise Transportation Co of Boston, USA to prove that gigantic steel sailing vessels with small crews were practical and economical alternatives to steam.

It is a dream that is still alive among marine architects today.

The Lawson *fully loaded in Boston harbour in 1906. Compare this with the photo of her unloaded on the previous page. In this picture, her hull has been painted black.*

A magnificent sight, but she handled like a beached whale

The seven-masted *Thomas W Lawson* was designed by Bowdoin B. Crowninshield and built in 1902 by the Fore River Ship and Engineering Company of Quincey, Massachusetts, USA for the sum of $258,000.

She was a magnificent sight; the largest fore-and-aft schooner that the world had ever seen – 5,128 tons, 376 feet long with a 50-foot beam.

She was the only seven-master ever constructed and the largest sailing ship ever built....

The seven masts were called Fore, Main, Mizzen, Number 4, Number 5, Number 6 and Spanker. However, the crew referred to them by the days of the week.

She carried 25 sails in all, 7 gaffsails, 7 topsails, 6 staysails and 5 jibs. The total sail area of 43,000 sq feet was equivalent to an acre and weighed 18 tons in all.

She was the only seven-master ever constructed and the largest sailing ship ever built. She had been originally designed to carry coal for the trans-Pacific trade, and was capable of loading over 9,000 tons. Later she was fitted out with internal tanks for 'black gold' – oil.

In 1906 at the Newport News Shipbuilding & Drydock Co she was rebuilt as a bulk oil-tanker. The topmasts were removed and the lower masts were used to vent the holds from oil gases.

Only when deeply loaded would she sail properly, but when full of cargo her draft exceeded that of almost all harbours where her cargo was needed. She was renowned as a poor sailer under almost all conditions.

A similar-sized steamship would have had a crew of up to 50 men, and a fully rigged sailing ship of the same period a crew of 28. Thanks to mechanical aids for sail handling, notably steam-driven donkey engines, the *Thomas W Lawson* needed a crew of only 18.

She was an economical wind-driven oil-tanker of impressive size that handled like a beached whale....

He wrote a novel called 'Friday the Thirteenth' that was published in November 1907.

A bizarre and curious co-incidence, as later events were about to prove.

he ship was named after Thomas William Lawson (1857–1925), an extraordinary and flamboyant Edwardian financier and oil company speculator from Boston, Massachusetts.

Lawson was famous for his readable books and magazine articles about finance and the Stock Market in which he castigated banks and large corporations.

After spending a large part of his fortune promoting his crusade on behalf of the common man, and failing to get President Theodore Roosevelt's attention, he returned to gambling on the Stock Market.

This eccentric and larger-than-life son of Boston was probably flattered to have such a radically designed vessel, the largest sailing ship ever built, named after him.

Thomas Lawson also wrote a novel called *Friday the Thirteenth* that was published in November 1907. A bizarre and curious co-incidence, as later events were to prove.

The start of the fateful voyage from Philadelphia to London

On 20 November 1907, under charter to the Anglo-American Oil Company and with a full cargo of 60,000 barrels of crude oil, the *Thomas W Lawson* slipped her moorings in Philadelphia harbour and set sail for London. The forecast was bad, and they ran into storms almost immediately.

Nineteen days later, on Monday 9 December a hard southerly gale sprung up which lasted throughout Tuesday and Wednesday. The ship was raked by massive seas and everything on deck was smashed, including all the lifeboats. Most of her canvas was shredded or carried away – she had just six sails left – and many of her hatches were stove in.

Unlucky Friday the Thirteenth

On the afternoon of Friday 13 December, in filthy weather, they sighted land and what appeared to be another sailing ship. The 'ship' turned out to be the Bishop Rock lighthouse, but by the time they realised it, they were already east of the lighthouse and in big trouble.

They were trapped in the Western Rocks without room to wear or enough canvas to tack. Captain Geoffrey Dow recognised the extreme danger of his position and decided to drop anchor and wait. They were in Broad Sound, inside the Bishop and between Gunner and Nundeep Rocks. A severe north-westerly gale was blowing and the seas were mountainous.

The keepers of the Bishop Light immediately saw the peril in which the *Thomas W Lawson* lay.

The gale was increasing as the lighthouse men signalled St Agnes and raised the alarm....

The St Agnes lifeboat is launched

The men of St Agnes launched the lifeboat at 4 pm and reached the *Thomas W Lawson* an hour later.

Incredibly, Captain Dow declined their offer of assistance. But they stood by anyway, making fast to her stern, and were later joined by the St Mary's lifeboat.

Convinced that he had faced worse storms than this in America, Captain Dow decided to ride it out, although eventually he requested that a local pilot come aboard. 'I guess I'm alright where I am' he said.

Islander Billy Cook Hicks, a Trinity House pilot, boarded the *Lawson* from the St Agnes lifeboat.

The St Agnes lifeboat

The St Mary's lifeboat then broke her mast while manoeuvring under the counter of the *Lawson*. She returned to St Mary's for repairs and to telegraph for tugs to come out from Falmouth on the mainland.

It was then discovered that W F Hicks, one of the St Agnes lifeboat crew, had come out without oilskins and was suffering from extreme hypothermia. It was decided to return with him to St Agnes.

Billy Cook Hicks stayed on board the *Lawson* with strict instructions to light a flare should further assistance be required.

But no one had informed the St Mary's lifeboat that the St Agnes boat had returned to her station on St Agnes....

'I guess I'm alright where I am....'

Captain Dow

A keen lookout is kept on St Agnes

The St Agnes lifeboatmen

They stayed up all night on St Agnes watching the pitching lights of the *Lawson* out in the Sound. At 2.30 am violent squalls and rainstorms cut visibility to a few hundred yards. When the squall cleared at 2.50 am no lights were any longer visible from the *Thomas W Lawson*.

They desperately hoped that the lights had been temporarily extinguished by the squall, but at daybreak the terrible truth was apparent. All they could see was wreckage being tossed on the surface of the huge seas.

On St Agnes they were dumbstruck. A voice called for action. It was Freddie Cook Hicks, the son of the pilot they had left aboard the Lawson.

Eight men, five named Hicks, took the gig *Slippen* to search the rocks. They saw forms of men on the island of Annet, but on landing in huge seas at about 8 am they discovered them to be corpses lashed to wreckage.

The crew of the Slippen after searching for bodies

The crew of the Slippen

The search for survivors

On searching the island, they discovered the unconscious body of George Allen, a Battersea man, whom they managed to revive. He was suffering from exposure and broken ribs, and they rushed him back to St Agnes and a warm bed.

Later, two men were seen on Hellweathers Rocks. One was the Engineer, Edward Rowe of Boston, who was persuaded to tie a rope around himself and jump back into the sea to be pulled aboard the *Slippen*. His cries of agony were pitiful to hear. They took him to St Agnes before returning to save the other man, Captain Dow, who, Rowe had told them, was seriously injured.

Four men managed to get within yards of the injured man, but a gully separated them. It was young Freddie Cook Hicks who volunteered to swim to the injured man with a rope and bring him over.

The Captain, a very big man almost helpless with injury and exposure, needed three men to help him back to *Slippen*. He told them that at about 3 am huge waves swept many of the deck-hands into the sea. The squalls then snapped first one anchor cable, then the other. He ordered life jackets to be donned, and every man for himself. He took to the mizzen rigging with the pilot, engineer, mate and others, and had been in the sea for two hours before clambering onto the rock.

The crew of Slippen congratulated by Thomas Algernon (right)

The account of Engineer Edward Rowe of Boston, Massachusetts:

'When the cables parted, the Captain, Pilot, Mate and I climbed into the mizzen rigging, each with a fathom of rope..... When the ship struck I dropped onto the deck and the sea carried me overboard.

'I went under her quarter and passed right under her keel. I came up on the other side and found myself entangled in the rigging of the mast which had fallen overboard. I struggled for a very long time. I thought of giving up but at last by a supreme effort, I escaped and surfaced to find myself on top of a boiling sea.

'I clutched at a piece of wood and was carried some distance. I saw a man with a lifebelt on and I shouted to him but he took no notice. After a quarter of an hour, I saw the man again and induced him to come and hold the same piece of wood as myself.

'As we were washed along I felt another piece of wood rise between my legs and I wound my legs round it. I now felt certain of being saved, because it struck me that I was riding on a cross.

'The two of us were rushing straight at two large rocks with an opening between them. As we neared them, I released my hold on the cross piece and clung to the piece between my legs. I was lucky, the other man was not so lucky. I never saw him again.'

Aftermath

The *Lawson* had split between the sixth and seventh masts, and today the two halves lie a quarter of a mile apart.

The US Government and the *Lawson*'s owners awarded gold medals to the boat crews, and a gold watch to Freddie Cook Hicks.

The *Slippen* crew were invited to the Abbey to be congratulated in person by Thomas Algernon.

Scilly became the first place in the world to suffer major oil pollution; ironically from a sailing-ship wreck.

The inquest agreed that no lifeboat could have survived in the heavy seas after about midnight that night.

George Allen died of his injuries. The body of pilot Billy Cook Hicks, father of brave Freddie, was never found.

The wreck of the Thomas W Lawson *the next morning*

Foredeck of the Minnehaha

The Tenth Chapter

In which a transatlantic liner comes to grief on Scilly Rock in 1910, but all are saved and the islanders prosper

'Oh please Lord, let us pray for all at sea. But if there's got to be wrecks, please send them to we.'

The Atlantic Transport Line's **Minnehaha** *was carrying 171 crew, 66 passengers and 17,000 tons of cargo when she crashed into Scilly Rock in the fog on 19 April 1910.*

The story of the *Minnehaha* is a mixture of co-incidence, farce and a slight feeling that the ship was in some ways an unlucky vessel. However, the particular events of 19 April 1910 turned out well for everyone involved and the usual element of tragedy that accompanied shipwrecks on Scilly was entirely missing.

The Atlantic Transport Line was part of an American consortium backed by the financier, J P Morgan. By the turn of the century it had acquired both the Red Star Line and the White Star Line (later to build the *Titanic*).

J P Morgan's $13-million loan allowed the Atlantic Transport Line to order six large liners; four would be built at Harland and Wolff in Belfast and two in America.

The second liner to be finished in Belfast, for a cost of $1.4 million, was *Minnehaha*. She sailed on her maiden voyage to New York on 7 July 1900.

Almost immediately, she had a narrow escape in Channel fog, just missing the Chatham packet, *Lord Warden*. A month later on 18 September she struck and sank the New York Harbor Towing Company tug *American*, killing two of the crew.

On 27 December 1904, at anchor off Gravesend, *Minnehaha*'s stern was struck by the British steamer *John Sanderson*. Two years later, in October 1906, *Minnehaha* rammed the Cunarder *Etruria* as both vessels attempted to leave New York harbour in fog. On 17 April 1909, she grounded in the Gedney Channel, that forms the entrance to New York harbour.

Not the first *Minnehaha* wreck

Coincidentally, off St Mary's on 18 January 1874 another *Minnehaha* , an 845-ton cargo barque, was wrecked with the loss of ten members of her crew. She had been *en route* from Callao, Peru to Dublin *(photo, page 15)*.

Thirty-six years after that sad event, in the early morning of 19 April 1910, the second *Minnehaha* was only a mile away from where her namesake had been wrecked.

The weather had been fine when they left New York, but on 16 April they had run into thick fog that made observation impossible. In short they had no real idea where they were. Lookouts were posted and peered into the gloom hoping to catch a glimpse of the Bishop Light.

What the lookout saw next was horrifying: rocks and breakers passed close by to port. Before any action could be taken there was a long grating sound and the ship came to a sudden halt with a loud crash.

They were on the rocks just east of Scilly Rock. There was a long silence eventually broken by the sound of shouting as the passengers rushed up on deck in a panic.

Illustrations from the Company's brochure show a high level of furnishing in the Library [top], *Saloon* [above], *Smoking Room* [right] *and Foredeck* previous page].

A most friendly welcome on Bryher

The captain and crew did a good job in calming the passengers who all went back down below to get dressed, before mustering at the lifeboat stations in an orderly and courteous fashion.

Being Edwardian society, they dressed in fashionable sea-going attire before being lowered in the lifeboats without further drama.

By this time, boats from Bryher, the nearest island, had arrived and piloted the lifeboats safely to the island where they disembarked and were treated with great kindness and consideration. Being wrecked, declared one of the passengers, was the most agreeable way to arrive in England.

The passengers' praise for the islanders knew no bounds. Not only were they well looked after, their possessions and personal belongings were gathered up from their cabins and were returned to them in perfect order. Some passengers even resisted the Company's attempt to ship them to the mainland to continue their journey.

Hard aground on Scilly Rock

Once all the passengers were safely ashore with their possessions, attention turned to salvaging the ship.

The captain refused to accept that his vessel was a total loss and he organised the crew to work to save her. To stand any chance of being floated off on the next spring tide she would have to be lightened. This meant throwing almost the entire cargo overboard.

The islanders realised this as well, and were not slow in appreciating the rich salvage opportunities that this presented. Their enthusiasm was such that the captain drew his pistol in order to keep them at bay. Soon, however, the islanders and the captain arrived at an accommodation and everyone worked together, the islanders taking advantage where they could.

Minnehaha *aground, busy discharging cargo and pumping out her forward holds*

The New York Times carried detailed reports of the incident

'Scillonians have always been famous wreckers, but they will remember this as the greatest day in their history.'

The New York Times

"The Atlantic Transport Line liner Minnehaha, *which ran ashore early on Monday morning, disgorged part of her 17,000 tons of valuable cargo, all day long casting it upon the waters, to be gathered up by those who cared to take the trouble.*

"Farming and fishing were abandoned; school even was dismissed ... Huge cases containing automobiles and pianolas followed one another over the side, striking the water with a great splash. Sewing machines and clocks went with them, while Michigan furniture floated everywhere.

"Many bales of cigarettes covered the face of the water, and tons of cheap American novels drifted to the nearby shore of Bryher. One farmer, more fortunate than the rest, had a big motor car on the deck of his craft, and several cases of sewing machines."

Jessie Mothersole, an islander who became well-known as a writer, archaeologist and historian, reported the words of a friend who was there:

'Motor-cars and grand-pianos are towed in – in cases. I believe a grand piano loose is of a sulky nature when in the sea, and instead of allowing itself to be towed it does its best to settle down comfortably at the bottom, and takes the boat with it if the rope is not quickly cut –

at least that is one experience of which I was told.

'The boats arrive laden with everything under the sun – clocks, and food, and anti-pain tablets, squirts, dress-lengths, wheels, typewriters, sewing-machines, phonographs, boxes of jewellry, boxes of oranges, barrels of apples, pencils, meat-skewers, and lots of tobacco and cigarettes.

'The policeman is kept quite busy trying to puzzle out the contents of the different boxes. One lady has lost a £1,500

motor-car. They say the value of the cargo is greater than that of all Scilly and Penzance put together.

'There is some indignation amongst the men, as they have only been offered £2 a head for the cattle they saved, and last time they had £5; and they say these are larger and were more difficult to save.

'What with the custom-house officers, salvage men, and police it is very difficult to smuggle anything, and so far I have only managed a pencil....'

Saving the cattle

The cargo included 234 cattle. The only way of getting them out was to force each animal to jump from cargo ports high up in the ship.

The terrified animals hit the water with a great splash and had to be lassooed and either tied to a boat or towed astern to the shore.. The gigs were pressed into service and did noble work bringing the animals in.

Of the animals on board 224 were salved in this way, only ten died.

SHIP SALVAGED, BACK IN SERVICE 5 MONTHS LATER, CAPTAIN SUSPENDED

The Engineering Superintendent of the Atlantic Transport Line went down to Scilly for ten days immediately after the accident to monitor the attempts to salvage the ship. He typed a detailed report and was not impressed with the operation.

But eventually on 11 May *Minnehaha* was successfully refloated after three weeks aground. Two days later she steamed under her own power to Falmouth with an escort of salvage vessels.

From there she went on to Southampton for repairs. Her damage proved not to be very serious and she was able to resume the London to New York service five months later on 27 October.

Despite a testimonial signed by the passengers arguing to the contrary, the Board of Trade blamed Captain Layland for the incident, and suspended his licence for three months.

CAPTAIN SYDNEY LAYLAND

In her memoir *Mark Twain and Me,* Dorothy Quick describes the unfortunate Captain Layland of the *Minnehaha* as being exceedingly tall. She had met him on Mark Twain's return from London aboard another Atlantic Transport Line ship and had been given a tour of the bridge and entertained to tea.

In 1910, when the *Minnehaha* wreck occurred, Layland was Commodore of the Line. By most standards, he was pretty accident-prone.

Under his command *Mobile* collided with *Corean* in December 1897. Layland was in charge when *Minnetonka* collided with a Runciman Line steamer off the Royal Sovereign Lightship in June 1902, which left her with a hole knocked into her port bow and her port anchor lost.

Minnetonka had another collision with the schooner *Sterling* in fog in 1907.

The *Minnehaha*'s next captain was the charismatic Claret....

Minnehaha continues her eventful life under Captain Claret

Unlike her sisters, *Minnehaha* was not requisitioned during the First World War but remained in company service under the command of Frank H. Claret. She became a well-known carrier of munitions.

In the summer of 1915 she had a fire on board caused by a time-bomb. It was brought under control by the crew before she had to put back to Halifax.

The New York Times reported that the device was set by Erich Muenter, a German sympathiser who had been living under various aliases since his 1906 indictment for poisoning his wife.

Muenter actively supported the German cause and specifically wanted J P Morgan to stop financing war loans to the European allies and supplying ammunition to them.

In 1915, he successfully detonated a bomb in the Capitol in Washington DC. He then travelled to Long Island to kidnap the younger J P Morgan's family, burst into the house and shot Morgan twice in the groin.

Although wounded, Morgan managed to wrestle his assailant to the floor and the butler then knocked Muenter senseless with a chunk of coal and the police were called.

They soon found the bomb-making equipment Muenter had obtained, but 50lbs of the 120lbs of dynamite that had been delivered to him could not be accounted for.

Under questioning, Muenter admitted that he had placed a bomb on a vessel that left New York the previous weekend (*Minnehaha* had sailed on Sunday, July 4). Wireless stations along the coast made desperate efforts to reach all ships at sea to warn them.

Skipper Claret was taking the *Minnehaha* to Britain with a heavy cargo of TNT. Several days out of New York he received a radiogram to the effect that a bomb hidden aboard his ship was timed to explode that very noon.

Captain Claret ordered the crew to make a search drill, but did not tell them why. When they failed to find anything, he stood anxiously on the bridge, and waited watch in hand.

A bomb on board

Noon came and went. Nothing happened. Claret had just about decided that it was a false alarm when at 12:30 the forward deck suddenly erupted.

By some miracle the bomb had been planted on top of a small amount of ordinary freight and had failed to set off the tons of TNT aboard. Captain Claret and the *Minnehaha* sailed safely on.

Minnehaha was eventually torpedoed off the Irish coast, and sunk by U48 12 miles from Fastnet, on 7 September 1917. *Minnehaha* was struck almost simultaneously amidships by torpedoes on either side and sank extremely rapidly, stern first, 'with her bow pointing like a column in the air'.

Claret had all 12 lifeboats ready to be lowered at a moment's notice but *Minnehaha* went down too quickly for any to be used. Blight, the 23-year old Marconi operator, was only able to send half of his distress call before the wireless room was submerged and he had to swim for it. He did not survive.

Claret saved 11 members of his crew by swimming with them to one of the rafts.

Forty-three men died in the incident, 12 of them officers, but 'many more would have been lost had it not been for the gallantry of Captain Claret'. A hundred men floated for more than an hour before a British patrol boat sighted them.

The skipper of the patrol boat recognised the *Minnehaha*'s captain in the water and boomed out: 'I say, is that you, Claret?' 'Aye, it's me!' Claret boomed back. Pneumonia nearly killed him shortly afterwards.

Acting on instructions from the president of the line, the local agent bought each man a new suit of clothes. The men were also paid an advance of £1, and from this made a collection and presented Captain Claret with a marble clock as a mark of their appreciation.

Minnehaha lies 12 miles south-east of the Fastnet Rock, sitting upright and mostly intact. The funnels and winches are clearly visible.

Salvage rights for the wreck were offered for sale in January 2007.

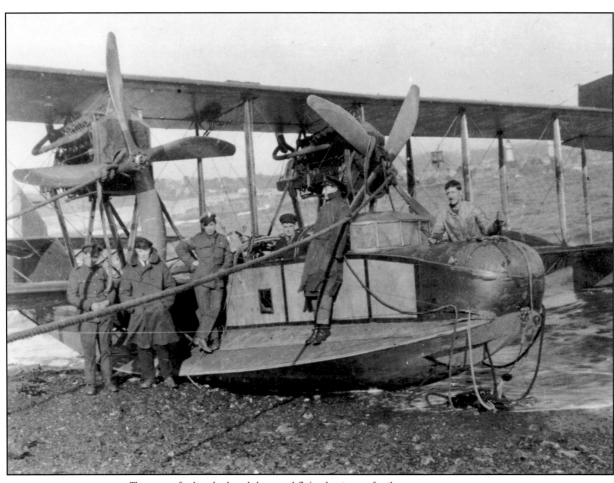

The crew of a beached and damaged flying-boat pose for the camera

The Eleventh Chapter

In which the island becomes a bastion of the Royal Navy in the fight against German U-boats

German U-boats tried to cut Britain's supply lifeline by torpedoing merchant ships in the Western Approaches...

After the Franco-Prussian war of 1870–71, Europe enjoyed 43 years of peace and prosperity.

In June 1914 Archduke Franz Ferdinand, heir to the Austro-Hungarian throne, was shot dead by a Serbian nationalist group. It was a shot heard around the world.

SS Eastgate torpedoed and aground off Tresco

Thomas Algernon was aged 68 when the Great War started.

In the 19th century, Scilly was saved from becoming a naval dockyard. The Royal Navy's latest weapon, the Dreadnought battleships, drew too much water to use Scilly as a harbour.

A new menace now threatened the nation – German submarines. To counter the U-boats a base was needed for seaplanes that could find the submarines and destroy them.

Scilly was the perfect place to build a Naval Air Station.

Tresco's involvement in the terrible Great War would be brief but effective. Royal Naval Air Station Tresco was created in 1917 and reached its zenith in the final days of the War, by which time it was a fully functional seaplane base with a vital anti-submarine role.

By the end of the war it had changed its name. In April 1918, the Royal Naval Air Service was merged with the Royal Flying Corps and the base ended its days as RAF Tresco.

The Great War of 1914–18 on Tresco

SS Great City *torpedoed and aground in Tresco Channel*

SS Gull Flight, *an American ship torpedoed off Scilly*

White Star Line Persic *torpedoed in September 1918 off Scilly*

In 1914, at the start of the Great War, Belgium fell to the Imperial German Army and Ostend and Zeebrugge became threatening bases for the German Navy.

As an island, Britain had to import vast quantities of food and raw materials by sea. Her survival depended on it. Germany's strategy was to cut off these sea-borne supplies. Their most effective weapon was the deadly U-boat.

By 1915, the German navy had sunk several British warships in home waters, including the battleship *Formidable* off the Dorset coast. Soon U-boats were operating in the Atlantic and Irish Sea. In one day, on 12 March that year, the German submarine U-29 sank four ships off Scilly.

The British response was to mount airship patrols to detect U-boats and bases were constructed on mainland Cornwall. In 1916 work was completed on Tresco to allow airships to moor between patrols, but the exposed nature of the site meant it was not used often.

Airships were proving effective on both sides. British airships drove off several U-boat attacks on convoys, while German Zeppelins bombed London and Liverpool.

Airship C9 photographed over Tresco early in the war

A seaplane base on Tresco becomes essential

In January 1917, it was decided to use float-planes against the U-boats and an experimental base was established at Porth Mellon on St Mary's. This proved too exposed, and operations were switched to the more sheltered New Grimsby harbour on Tresco.

At the same time, two destroyers arrived at Scilly to carry out trials on a man-carrying kite designed to be towed astern of a fast-steaming destroyer.

The idea was to raise an observer to detect U-boats, or other vessels over the horizon. It was a concept developed by Colonel 'Buffalo Bill' Cody from America. Various brave men volunteered to be lifted aloft but the concept never worked very well in practice.

A proposal to drop men silently at night behind enemy lines in Flanders from a man-carrying kite was tested elsewhere but sadly was never successful.

Conventional anti-submarine warfare was not enough.... A flying-boat base was needed.

This massive German mine was laid in the Western Approaches but washed ashore on Bryher without exploding.

The Royal Navy's destroyers and corvettes were trained to drop depth charges on any U-Boat located from the air.

The Great War of 1914–18 on Tresco

Eventually in 1917 it was decided to put Royal Naval Air Station Tresco on to a full operational footing. Tents were erected in the field at the bottom of the Abbey drive next to the Great Pool, and No 1 Air Construction Corps moved in.

Tents at the bottom of the Abbey Drive in New Grimsby

Air Construction Corps transport on Tresco outside the old Bothy. This later became an ammunition store and is now holiday cottages Puffin, Tern *and* Kittiwake

Permanent buildings, a metal hangar, canteen and a substantial slipway for the retrieval and launching of seaplanes were constructed. For the first time motorised transport ran on the roads of Tresco. The vehicles were marked ACC for the Air Construction Corps

Was there a last chivalrous moment in naval warfare?

It has often been claimed that the German High Command in both World Wars specifically forbade both the Luftwaffe and Krieg Marine from attacking Scilly or their supply ship as repayment for the islanders' kindness and sensitivity in helping the mostly German survivors of the *Schiller* disaster.

U-29 *alongside* SS Headlands whose *crew were allowed to leave in lifeboats before their ship was sunk.*

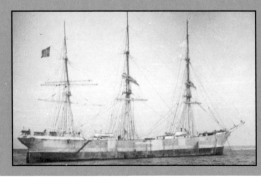

This Norwegian sailing ship was shelled by a U-boat but somehow survived.

It is a subject of much debate, but most people dismiss the idea as sentimental fantasy. A significant minority insist that it is true. Certainly, Scilly seemed to get off relatively lightly despite being a legitimate target.

Tresco starts to equip herself for war

A revolutionary floating refuelling dock for seaplanes was designed by one of the naval pilots, Edward Burling, who later achieved fame by becoming the first man ever to be catapulted in an aircraft from a ship.

But this would not happen until 1924 in *HMS Vindictive.*

A wireless station was also constructed on the island.

The Great War of 1914-18 on Tresco

Mr A E Bull had been a school-teacher before he was conscripted into the Royal Naval Air Service. Later in 1973, he wrote about helping to build RNAS Tresco in a letter to islander Roy Cooper. He also kept a photograph album, from which many of these pictures are taken.

'ctober of 1917 was when I first came to know Tresco, and it was in many ways my good fortune to be stationed there for fifteen months. I had joined the Royal Naval Air Service and after two months at a training camp in Norfolk, I was one of a draft sent to Tresco; a Cornish man at the camp told me that that it was one the islands in the Isles of Scilly.

'We were to join a larger force called the Construction Corps. Work was already in progress at New Grimsby on permanent quarters for men of the RNAS small seaplane base.

'Our section camped in bell tents near the sea but this proved too exposed and the camp was moved. The new site was a rectangular site south of the Great Pool; it was more sheltered and better laid out.

'The entrance, still there, sloped down and at an angle to the road. The trees on each side are probably successors to the more robust ones that I remember. Those at the eastern end of the field seem the same as the ones I knew. I sometimes walked through them to the Gardens.

'The view of the lake was as it is now, and I well remember how the islanders prophesied that we should all have rheumatism; fortunately, they were wrong.

'Our four lines of bell-tents ran parallel with the road beginning level with the entrance and running east, with I think six or eight in a line, and four men sleeping in each tent. To the left of the entrance was a large marquee that served as a meals tent.

'On the lake side of this was a wooden recreation hut; there may have even been two.

During the 1914-18 War a number of men of the Royal Naval Air Service were stationed on Tresco, then a small seaplane base. One section of these was a construction corps engaged upon building huts in concrete for more permanent living quarters etc. for the station. This section, (in which I served) was under canvas in the field south of the lake. This picture is a copy of a painting I made of the camp in 1918.

A E Bull
1972

'Technically, we were in the Navy and so had hammocks but since we could not 'sling' them we were entitled to sixpence a night 'hard lying' money which we duly received until later when we were merged with the RAF. Thin mattresses, blankets etc were part of our kit and many tents had wooden floors, so the lying was not specially hard!

'In the first December we were there a very fierce westerly wind struck the islands and almost flattened our camp. All through the night we strove to keep the guy-ropes tight, but some tent poles broke and by the morning most tents were flat, including the marquee.

'With the gale still blowing we were instructed to carry – a difficult job in the wind – camp equipment and our belongings to a large barn in New Grimsby which had a good upper floor, and this had to be our "home" for a while.

'Two large flying-boats, built in mahogany marine plywood were anchored off Bryher in Cromwell Sound. There had not been time to get them onto the slipway, and the wind flung them about until they broke up completely. The engines sank and for weeks afterwards we could pick up bits of plywood on the island shores. A naval motor launch rode out the storm away from the coast and rocks.

'In due course the camp was re-conditioned and improved. The tents, arranged as before, had each a circle of ground around them and the walking space was sanded. The perimeter fencing was covered with vertical bunches of rushes – on the advice, I believe, of the very knowledgeable islanders who were expert in screening their daffodil fields. Above

Aerial view of New Grimsby in 1917. The hangar has its struts and foundation in place, the slipway is in place and the accommodation huts are finished.

'Two large flying-boats, built in mahogany marine plywood were anchored in Cromwell Sound and the wind flung them about until they broke up completely.'

this, on tall uprights wire netting was stretched – surprising to us – for a further windbreak. Certainly the camp remained intact afterwards.

'It was from this camp that the working parties emerged each morning through the gateway to the road, turning right and passing between two banks of New Zealand flax on the way to the site which was being prepared or on which huts were being erected.

A flying-boat wrecked by high winds in Cromwell Sound

By the end of the war, a large maintenance hangar had been built with ancillary stores and accommodation huts

'The site I think must have been somewhere near where the present builders yard is. It had to be levelled and one considerable hillock of sand required the use of tip-trucks and light 'railway lines' to be transported elsewhere to build up levels.

'The huts were built of concrete which was mixed on a 'banker-board' by hand – we did not have a mechanical mixer – and taken in wheel-barrows to a 'Winget' machine and put into a mould for the type of block required, and then rammed down. Pulling a lever let down the iron sides of the mould leaving the new block on an iron plate ready to be carried to storage space to harden.

'In hut construction rectangular blocks with slots at each end built up the uprights down the sides, while L-shaped ones, also with slots, formed the corners. Both types had holes for reinforcing rods or 'grouting' with concrete slabs 2½ ins thick cast in moulds were lowered into the slots, thus forming walls with spaces left for doors and windows.

'Concrete also being used for floors and paving, there was a great demand for cement. This in 2-cwt sacks was brought by small ships, usually herring drifters in Government service. These could only berth at New Grimsby Quay at high tide and had to be unloaded without delay to enable the vessel to leave again.

Making friends with the islanders

'The unfortunate company on duty at the time turned out for the job of unloading cement and other supplies whatever the time of day or night.

'There was a store, brick-built I think, at the shore end of the Quay near where the little Quay Shop is now, and we had some small lorries for transport. These and a small Ford car for other uses were the only motor vehicles on the island, and the position was much the same on St Mary's.

'From New Grimsby Quay or from Carn Near (without a jetty as there is now) we could, when off-duty, go in the 'liberty boat' to Hugh Town, much smaller and quieter that it is now. But time did not allow much exploration. It had to be remembered that we were not on holiday, and it was wartime – affecting civilians as well as those in the Services. I was never able to visit St Agnes, although I have since.

'Unless we were on duty much of evening time was free and part of Sundays. Some of the men had, or could borrow, a boat for a trip to Bryher. Teas at cottages were sometimes possible, but food rationing was a restriction.

'Three friends and I bought an elderly but still serviceable boat in Hugh Town, but kept it on the Old Grimsby shore, and so had St Martin's for our visits, having with caution and advice learnt our way. Sometimes an evening's fishing would add pollock or mackerel (if we had been lucky) to our or someone else's service rations.

'Living almost entirely on Tresco it was fortunate if one could find interests of one's own making; the population, apart from service personnel, was small. I can only remember one general shop, and food was rationed. There was, of course, no cinema and radio in the home was still some years away.

'But at least some of us made friendly contact with the people of Tresco. As a teacher myself, I sought out the headmistress of the small school to share interests. She invited four of us to the schoolhouse where she lived with her mother. I have forgotten her name.

'We were sometimes able to use her piano for a little not-very-expert music, but very welcome to camp dwellers. On rare occasions we had a church parade and St Nicholas church, and the Vicar kindly agreed to my occasionally using the church organ for an hour or two – with the help of a boy living nearby to "blow" for me. It was a very small pipe organ with some peculiar features but very welcome to me.

'Other help came from the bailiff, as I think he was called. From him I was offered the use of

Sea-plane in a flat calm sea at Old Grimsby

'I sought out the headmistress of the small school to share interests. She invited four of us to the schoolhouse where she lived with her mother.'

Cottages in Old Grimsby – since demolished

part of his office, out of working time, as a dark room. I had a little folding 'plate' camera – there were no military secrets there! – and I took a few pictures of the flower growing and such subjects as might be of interest later.

'Some photographic supplies and some good postcards could be bought at the Chemist in Hugh Town where the present one still stands. You may be amused to hear of another service we had from the bailiff. Somewhere on the farm he showed us a rectangular pig trough scrubbed very clean, and he offered it to us as a substitute for a bath; a welcome one for tent dwellers. I forget how hot water was obtained.

'From various people we learned much about the flower-growing and were able to watch one whole season through with much interest and pleasure.

'The undertaking seemed to involve most of the people, certainly on Tresco. I remember the picking in the bud stage, the distribution with horse and cart to the cottages, the skillful grouping, and then the final packing into cardboard boxes in a long glass-house. They were then ready for transport to St Mary's quay and the boat for Penzance – a predecessor of the *Scillonian* (was it the *Lyonesse*?).

'It must be remembered that what I saw was under wartime conditions and restrictions, and doubtless with young men in the Forces. The German submarines were sinking ships in the approaches to Britain; they probably treated the dangerous waters around Scilly with respect. Our small seaplane base was doubtless intended for reconnaissance, and there was a store of bombs – small ones for the seaplanes to carry – and I remember that the north end of Samson was used for target practice, sometimes with live bombs.
'There was not much level ground where ordinary planes could land but I remember that once, to our great interest, a very small airship came from the mainland and landed at Tresco.

Mr Kelloway and Mrs Vernon picking

Islanders Kelloway and Goddard distributing the flowers to islanders' cottages for bunching

RNAS Tresco is completed

Accommodation huts in New Grimsby

The elongated balloon had slung underneath it a small platform with safety 'walls' (metal network probably) and on this was space for the pilot and one other, plus the motor to drive the propeller.

'It must have been in the middle of 1918 that work on a fairly large hangar was begun. The slip is still there. The concrete bases for many of the hut still remain.

'It was a framework of iron girders and the foundations for the main uprights were based upon large concrete cubes (about 5 feet) filling spaces dug in the ground (mostly sand). There must have been qualified people in the Construction Corps and workmen able to tackle the placing and bolting together of the girders.

'I know that one man who previously had been working with a horse and cart proved to be a surveyor who then became responsible for accurate structural measurements.

'Another project which was begun and never finished was for a railway line from the quay in New Grimsby to the buildings. Ordinary rails and wooden sleepers began arriving and had to be unloaded and stacked even after the end of the War. What happened to these, I wonder?

'I have so far made no reference to the fact that while these things were happening in these fairly remote islands, the war with its ghastly long lists of casualties was raging in France and elsewhere, and the outcome remained in doubt certainly for the first part of the year.

The Great War of 1914–18 on Tresco

The ship's company of Royal Naval Air Station Tresco pose in front of the hangar

'With radio then no more than messages in Morse Code and with newspapers not readily available, we listened to news or rumour which reached us perhaps from those who had been on leave or more directly when, at long intervals, we ourselves went. After July news brought more hope, but not until October was there talk of an armistice.

'But at home another scourge became widespread through the country in a very serious epidemic of influenza causing a large number of deaths. In spite of the distance from the mainland the disease reached Scilly and numbers of men succumbed to it – in a few cases fatally. How it affected the islanders themselves I do not know.

'But by now victory seemed certain and on November 11th at 11 o'clock in the morning an Armistice was signed, and the news soon reached us. It was my first day out-of-doors after being in 'sick bay' with influenza and I saw slung between the two tall wireless masts the message in naval signal flags saying (I was told) "Peace with Victory".

'The work we were doing now seemed pointless though some supplies (including the rails) for the work continued to arrive, but by January demobilisation was beginning.

'On a wet morning in January 1919 I left Tresco from Carn Near to board a steamer at St Mary's to begin my journey home. It was

The original caption to this photo reads: 'Tresco's champion 'bus' Fililu. This plane held the war record for distance covered'.

not until April 1972 that I landed again, with much interest, at the same point. It was then my pleasure to act as guide to my family party.

'Tresco was much as, over the years, I remembered it and the views in so many directions remain unchanged, though my memory has been refreshed. As always the light, colours, mist and brightness are continually changing and the moods vary from the scowl of storm clouds to the glory of sunset colours reflected on calm seas between the islands.'

A E Bull
Tenby, Pembrokeshire
(formerly of Surrey) **1973**

'On a wet morning in January 1919 I left Tresco from Carn Near to board a steamer at St Mary's to begin my journey home....'

It was early in 1917 when Squadron Commander Hope-Vere moved operations from Porth Mellon on St Mary's to New Grimsby on Tresco.

RNAS Tresco started flying missions in February 1917 with six H-12 flying boats. Many of the station staff were still billeted on St Mary's, while others, like A E Bull, occupied tents, before eventually moving into wooden huts on Tresco.

In July 1917, Tresco suffered a tragic setback when an ammunition store exploded in the Bothy *(now holiday cottages Puffin, Tern and Kittiwake)* next to New Grimsby beach. Three men were killed and several injured. The men were on the beach, possibly arming bombs, when the explosion occurred.

A tragic accident on Tresco

The Bothy after the explosion. This was taken from the beach where the three men were arming bombs

Damage was extensive. This is the other side of the Engine Shed, now Old Mill. The propellors were salvaged along with other spare parts

Blast damage at the side of the Engine Shed

Work started on rebuilding, and the Bothy was finished five months later

A team of three armament artificers, photographed at RNAS Tresco about the time of the tragedy. The photo belongs to Ray Holder of Bournemouth, whose father Albert W Holder stands on the left in this picture

All resources brought to bear against the U-boats

Drifters at St Mary's. Fishermen and their boats were used to patrol the Western Approaches, as back-up to the Navy

By 1917 aircraft from Tresco were patrolling an area that extended 85 miles south-west of Scilly. They were assisted by a fleet of drifters that did duty as patrol boats crewed by fishermen.

By the beginning of 1918 two-thirds of British ships sunk had been torpedoed within 10 miles of the coast. The convoy system was designed to bunch ships together and therefore to leave large sectors of the ocean empty. The frustrated German submarines were forced to take up operational station nearer the convoys' destination in order to have the chance of a target, thus presenting themselves as a target for RNAS Tresco's aircraft.

Sea-planes from Tresco were soon in action against the U-boats. In May 1917 one of the H-12s attacked a German submarine on the surface that had been damaged in an earlier attack. The plane's two bombing runs were

unsuccessful, all the bombs missing. The Germans, in this instance, proved to be particularly tough prey, using their deck gun to fire at the aircraft and scoring a hit on the plane's starboard engine.

The engineer climbed out on the wing to carry out a temporary repair to the leaking radiator, and they duly returned safely to Tresco.

Just three days later a sister aircraft from Tresco sank a submarine with a direct hit forward of the conning tower. All the plane's crew received medals. This was the first success anywhere in the world by a plane against a U-boat.

Tresco aircraft continued to carry out many missions against U-boats, as well as mine clearing. The latter task consisted of machine-gunning the floating mines from the air – simple and effective.

Plumb Island, New Grimsby

It was no easy job keeping the ship's company of several hundred young men occupied and happy while living on a small island remote from the usual amusements of the mainland.

Sports Days were a popular summer activity that engendered keen competition between the different departments.

They were organised with a lot efficiency; running tracks and field events were properly marked out and a loudspeaker commentary and a refreshment tent were provided.

They were also popular with islanders and provided a welcome break for everyone from the monotony of wartime work.

The 1917 Engineers football team *[above]* was photographed at Valhalla and was presumably drawn from the artificers at RNAS Tresco. The Army team of the same name – the Royal Engineers – had competed successfully in the FA Cup before the Great War. The Sappers were finalists in 1872, 1874 and 1878 and won it in 1875. This photograph came up for auction in Truro and was bought by Euan Rodger, the island's current hotel manager.

The artificers in uniform *[below]* were also photographed in 1917. The photo comes from Dr Martland whose great-great-uncle sits on the extreme right in the back row. His name was Emerson Lowe.

Private Walter Franklin

In any church in Britain you will see war memorials on which are inscribed the names of local people who died in action. St Nicholas church on Tresco is no different, and is particularly poignant because of the terrible toll paid by the Dorrien Smith family.

Among the names of other islanders who lost their lives is that of Private Walter Franklin who served in the Duke of Cornwall's Light Infantry during the Great War. His is a small piece of history that illuminates just one name on the plaque in St Nicholas church.

Walter Franklin worked as a baker on Tresco and he was comparatively old at 38 when he left Tresco for St Mary's on a sunny summer's day. He took the steamer to Penzance and enlisted at the recruiting office on 15 June 1916. Exactly a week later he was on another island – Freshwater on the Isle of Wight – for basic infantry training.

Later, he was posted to D Company, 7th (Service) Battalion of the Duke of Cornwall's Light Infantry. He served at the Front and was killed in action at Saillisel, Somme on 17 January 1917 – almost seven months to the day after he enlisted.

Walter must have felt a long way from home that day. It was bitterly cold and 4 inches of snow had fallen overnight. It was like nothing he'd ever experienced in the mild climate of Tresco. It coated everything – and for a while the hideous brown mud lay under a white blanket.

At 6 o'clock that morning the German guns opened up and laid down a barrage on the British lines where D Company had their position. They sheltered in their dug-outs and trenches, ready to repel an enemy attack that often followed such a barrage.

Sure enough, the Germans came at them, firing and hurling grenades. The Cornishmen of C and D Company stood firm, the German attack was repulsed and the line was held. But at a price.

Eight men were badly wounded in C Company and one man, Private Hoskings, was killed. D Company lost one man killed – Private Walter Franklin from Tresco.

At 5.30 that afternoon, the Cornishmen were relieved by the 12th Battalion King's Liverpool Regiment, and they left the Front to rest behind the lines.

Walter Franklin is remembered with honour on memorials on Scilly, and his name is inscribed on the Thiepval Memorial among those of 73,357 British and South African comrades who have no known grave and who fell on the Somme. It is the largest British war memorial anywhere in the world.

St Nicholas Church – as Walter Franklin would have known it. He and others from Tresco who died in the Great War are commemorated there

A LOVELY LIFE..... Islander Albert Steel, aged 90, looks back

I was bom on Tresco in 1909, I am the youngest son of Frederick and Alice Louise. All my family worked for the Dorrien Smiths, my father was a top gardener in their employment. I had three brothers in the 1914–18 War. Fred the eldest won the Military Medal, Edward lost a leg, and Arthur the youngest was killed.

My grandmother was the Housekeeper to the Dorrien Smiths who thought very highly of her, they had surgeons come to Tresco to operate on her when she had cancer. She lived until she was 80 years old. Her tombstone is in the churchyard.

It was a lovely life on the island. We were poor but healthy. We made up for it by having our own boat and going fishing for pollock, mackerel and many other fish – including spearing plaice. When the tide was out we caught scallops, cockles and winkles. We had our own shrimping nets, it was a lovely life.

During the 1914–18 War we used to get up early in the morning to see what had washed ashore from wrecks blown up by the German U-boats. The story goes, I'm told it's true, the Germans never touched the islands because we buried some that had drowned. They are buried on St Mary's.

The five inhabited islands were St Mary's, St Martin's, St Agnes, Bryher and Tresco. Tresco being the best. My father was in charge of all the greenhouses, growing peaches, nectarines, grapes and other exotic plants. The climate was good for early flowers which were sent to the mainland for sale.

When I was a boy the islands were so thinly populated that we knew everyone on all five islands. We used to have gig races between the islands. All my brothers and sisters used to row in the boats, competing against boats from other islands.

Looking back to the 1914–18 War we had a seaplane base on Tresco some of the personnel used to lodge with us and take part in the Gig Races.

Unfortunately, there was an accident when a man on the base was doing something to a bomb when it exploded killing and injuring some. They turned the Working Men's Club and Reading Room into a hospital....

'Boom' Trenchard, known as the Father of the RAF and a close relative of the Dorrien Smiths, visited Tresco by flying-boat

The Twelfth Chapter

*In which, as the Great War ends
'The Major' becomes Proprietor,
and Tresco Abbey Garden
becomes one of the world's great
horticultural treats*

Major A A Dorrien Smith
1876–1955

Proprietor from 1918

***Following the Great
War life in Britain, and
on Tresco, changed for
ever. The old order
was gone and new
ideas and methods had
to be employed.***

***Arthur Algernon was
the right man for the
time...***

Arthur Algernon – Major A A Dorrien Smith – was aged 42 when his father Thomas died at the end of the First World War. 'The Major' had had a distinguished army career by the time he became the new Proprietor.

From birth he had grown up among exotic plants on Tresco and he had always embraced the opportunities for travel that the Army offered. Apart from anything else it gave him a chance to collect plants from around the world while serving the King.

He served in South Africa between 1899 and 1902 and diligently sent back plants to his father on Tresco. In 1903 he was appointed ADC to the Governor-General of Australia, and helped to set up the Botanic Garden in Melbourne.

Next, as a Captain, he joined a scientific expedition to the Auckland and Campbell Islands off the coast of New Zealand.

After marrying Eleanor Bowlby he took his young bride to Perth and Albany in Western Australia. It was an uncomfortable and rugged trip, but one that they both enjoyed since Eleanor was herself a keen plantswoman.

Together the newlyweds excitedly gathered strange and wonderful species to plant in the temperate climate of Tresco. Mostly, they were successful in transplanting their exotica in Scilly from the other hemisphere, exactly the opposite side of the globe.

They were inspired to write a paper about their trip for the Royal Horticultural Society – 'A Botanising Expedition to Western Australia in the Spring'.

Plants were not the only exotica that he brought back from the Southern Hemisphere. Birds were hauled back to Tresco to join the 'Duckery' – well stocked with rare ducks and swans, and also with rhea from New Zealand.

The First World War took Arthur Algernon away from Tresco, along with the 92 other Tresco men and women who served their country. His return in 1918 was not the joyful occasion it should have been, coinciding as it did with the death of his father.

In his absence during the War, the flower and potato industry had declined and was barely a profitable proposition anymore. Like so much else on the mainland, society had changed forever; the happy abandon of the Edwardian Age had been replaced with sombre reality.

For Arthur Algernon – 'The Major' as he was known – it meant facing the fact that he could no longer afford to run the five inhabited islands of Scilly as his father had done before the War. Four years after inheriting the lease, he returned responsibility and control of all the islands – except for Tresco and the uninhabited islands – to the Duchy.

He retained his position, however, as Chairman of the Isles of Scilly Council and held it for his lifetime.

Tresco Abbey Garden continued to go from strength to strength under the Major's guidance. There were 16 gardeners employed to create and maintain not just the exotic plants but also the peaches, melons and nectarines that were cultivated in the great glasshouses.

The Major was a plantsman of great repute and enthusiasm and introduced hundreds of the species that can be seen today. By 1935 the first list of plants of Tresco exceeded 3,500.

There were sixteen gardeners employed to create and maintain not just the exotic plants but also the peaches, melons and nectarines that were cultivated in the great glasshouses.

Island summers

The child is Helen Dorrien Smith who today has a house on Tresco

Summers were spent riding, boating, picnicking and attending events such as the island Fete. The winter provided good shooting, including the traditional shoot on the uninhabited islands in December.

The traditional December shoot on the uninhabited islands

Nature was not kind....

Between the wars, Nature was not kind. In 1929 110 mile-an-hour winds ripped through the Garden devastating the plants and uprooting trees. The wind changed direction three times tearing into plants and knocking over 600 mature trees.

It was a disaster, but with it came an unexpected bonus – new areas of the garden were now sunnier than before, and a programme of replanting established an even finer plant collection and a more open design.

In 1936 more storms and heavy rain caused severe flooding in Old Grimsby to a degree not seen since.

Arthur Algernon Dorrien Smith

The First World War had advanced the aviation industry and in the period immediately afterwards civilian aviation started to develop rapidly.

It remained, however, a past-time of the rich. Learning to fly and then owning an aircraft was, and still is, an expensive pastime. Neither was airline travel cheap. Passengers paid heavily to fly anywhere and the days of cheap air travel for the masses was still half a century away.

The Isles of Scilly and in particular the generously hospitable Dorrien Smiths became an exciting destination for private aviators. Various planes made the trip either landing on Pentle Bay beach, St Mary's golf course or, in the case of seaplanes, in St Mary's Roads.

Eugene de Veance landed this Farman-Samson monoplane on Pentle beach in July 1935. Islanders pulled it up to Valhalla – close to what is now the heliport – where it was parked until he left the island a few days later. The plane was pushed back to Pentle beach and refuelled before making a successful flight back to France

Dropping in by plane....

In June 1932, a Puss Moth landed successfully on St Mary's Golf Course

Left: *Flying boat Calcutta arrived in 1928, as did 'Boom' Trenchard [below] who was a close relative of the Dorrien Smiths. He was rowed ashore at Carn Near*

The Flight of *COLUMBIA*

October 1930

On 9 October 1930, a small Bellanca monoplane took off from Harbour Grace in Newfoundland, Canada. Twenty-three hours later it landed at Pentle Bay, 'near the small coastal town of Tresco' according to the pilot's log.

The 1920s and '30s were an exciting time for long distance aviation. In 1919 the first Atlantic crossing had been achieved by Alcock and Brown for Britain in a Vickers Vimy biplane.

In May 1927 Lindbergh crossed the Atlantic, and a few weeks later the feat was repeated by the Americans Chamberlin and Levine in *Columbia*.

Columbia was then sold to J Errol Boyd, a former Royal Canadian Air Force pilot from Montreal who, together with Lieutenant R P Connor of the United States Navy as navigator, set off from Montreal to fly the Atlantic on behalf of Canada.

In 1933 the Prince of Wales visited Scilly to meet islanders and was escorted on a tour of the islands by Arthur Algernon.

The flight of *Columbia*

Bad weather forced them down on Prince Edward Island before they flew on to Harbour Grace to start their Atlantic flight. Although *Columbia* was still painted on the plane, Boyd had renamed her *Maple Leaf* and had painted one on her fuselage.

They took off on 9 October 1930 at 16.30 and expected to land at Croydon Airport near London just over a day later.

However, as they approached Scilly after 23½ hours they started to experience problems with the fuel supply and decided to land.

After a short search for a suitable landing site, Boyd decided on the sand of Pentle Bay and made a successful landing.

They found that a blocked fuel pipe had caused the trouble, and this was soon cleared.

On Tresco they were put up at the Abbey by the Major while the RAF from Mount Batten supplied them with some aviation fuel.

They were able to take off the following day for Croydon where a large crowd greeted them enthusiastically at the end of the first transatlantic flight by a Canadian.

On 22 December 1939, three days before
Christmas, the British cargo ship SS
Longships *was wrecked on the Seven
Stones just off Scilly in the exact spot that
the* Torrey Canyon *would meet her end on
18 March 1967. All the crew were rescued.*

The shadow of war

From the moment that he inherited Tresco in 1918, Arthur Algernon – The Major – had devoted himself tirelessly to ensuring that the island could survive economically.

The cut-flower industry on the island had been put onto a commercial footing and, as an enthusiastic plant-collector, he had encouraged and directed the re-planting of the Abbey Garden after the dreadful storms that ripped them apart.

He also had the foresight to encourage the use of pilot gigs even though reliable marine combustion engines seemed to make rowing-boats redundant.

It was the tragic shipwreck of the *Isabo* in 1927 that showed how, at times, rowing boats were more effective than motor-boats when it came to saving men's lives at sea.

The Major and the Home Guard on parade

In the early 1930s, in the middle of the Jazz Age, a man who would change everyone's life was elected to power in Germany.

Shortly after Adolf Hitler's invasion of Poland, Britain was at war.

With the Abbey Garden staff substantially reduced because of war service, the Major spent a great deal of his time personally tending the plants in between taking charge of the Home Guard.

His wife Eleanor, with whom he had shared so many plant-collecting trips, took charge of the Garden, the island hospital and a detachment of Land Girls.

Tresco's Home Guard

How the S.S. ISABO looked at dawn
28 Oct 1927.   photo. King & Son. Scilly

This painting is by lifeboatman Harry Barrett. The Isabo *crew member saved by Janey Slaughter later remarked that two stern masts were missing in the painting, but they may have been lost in the incident.*

Shipwreck! The *Isabo*

The Thirteenth Chapter
*In which the Italian cargo
ship* Isabo *founders on Scilly
Rock. Six seamen are lost
but thirty-two are saved by
heroic islanders*

'A terrible scene
confronted us....
The cries of the
men in the water
were pitiful to
hear.'

**On 27 October 1927,
the SS Isabo struck
Scilly Rock on a
foggy night at 5 pm.
She promptly split
in two just forward
of the funnel**

*Harry Barrett was a crewman in the lifeboat, and he painted this
picture of the* Isabo *as they found her on the day of the wreck*

The *SS Isabo*, 6,827 tons, had been built at
the start of the Great War in 1914 at
Trieste. Her triple expansion engines gave
her a modest speed of around 12 knots.
She was in her thirteenth year and on her way from
Montreal to Hamburg with a cargo of grain with a
crew of 38 Italians and Estonians.

On Bryher they heard a ship's siren that dense,
foggy afternoon. It was bleating like a lost sheep.
They knew that a ship was in serious danger. She
sounded close and that meant she was already
amongst the most dangerous rocks in the world....

They launch the *Czar*

So they opened the gig shed doors, and readied the pilot gig *Czar* for sea. Seven oarsmen and a coxswain were the crew.

Norman Jenkins was in his 20s at the time, and half a century later he taped his memories for posterity:

> 'We went out in the Czar *from Great Porth and when we got inside Scilly (Rock) we came on the wreckage with the men scattered through it amongst all this timber.*
>
> 'The ship had broken in two as she struck.... The timber was 27 feet and 8 by 5 inches and was used for keeping her cargo of grain from shifting. There must have been an acre – even an acre and a half – of this timber, tanks also, and casks.'

> '*The cries of the men in the water were pitiful to hear....*'

Another of the gig crew that dreadful evening was a temporary resident – the Baptist Minister The Rev E R Pearce. His memories stayed with him forever:

> *A terrible scene confronted us.... huge iron tanks, broken boats, hatches, planks, spars etc. drifted on the surface, while scattered here and there among the ruins could be seen the head and shoulders of men clinging to the broken pieces of timber for support.*
>
> '*The cries of the men in the water were pitiful to hear.... they were so poorly clad that we had little to assist them by.*'

Gigs and motor-boats save lives...

The *Czar* fights to save lives

The *Czar* doggedly continued in her task of saving lives in the fog, assisted by two motor boats from Bryher – the *Ivy* and *Sunbeam* – which arrived after making their way round from the other side of the island via Shipman's Head and through Hell Bay.

Young Norman Jenkins never forgot what he saw that afternoon:

'The worst of it was that some of them had nothing on but a vest or a shirt. You didn't know how to grip them...'

'We took 14 men from the water, and the last one off the ship. When we had 11 on the Czar we didn't know how many more we would get, so we freed the gig for more by putting them on board of the Ivy and then went back and got four more aboard.

'There were some men on the Isabo's cross-tree. It wasn't possible to get to them or to the mate who had swum to Scilly Rock.

'The worst of it was that some of them had nothing on but a vest or a shirt. You didn't know how to grip them. But we managed!

'There was one funny thing. We put one of them in the bottom of the gig and he put this bucket on his head. It seemed awfully funny to see him sitting there with a bucket on his head!'

The motor-boats cannot continue

Both the two motor boats, the *Ivy* and *Sunbeam,* started encountering real problems.

The spilled grain clogged their circulating pipes and the engines became red-hot. So the *Sunbeam* launched a small 8-ft dinghy which was responsible for bringing in twelve men.

At one stage, a rope thrown to the wreck had five desperate seamen clinging to it.

That afternoon there was hardly a Bryher islander – or a Jenkins or a Pender – that was not afloat.

The St Mary's lifeboat – the *Elsie*, with Matt Lethbridge at the helm – was faced with a terrible dilemma when it eventually reached the scene....

Men were known to be in the fore-rigging of the *Isabo*. It was the only place they could go as the heaving seas covered with heavy planks and metal tanks would have crushed them.

But now conditions had become appalling – darkness, lumpy seas, floating wreckage –and on top of everything, the lifeboat's propellors became fouled by a floating mattress.

The coxswain, reluctantly but with sound judgement, decided to wait until daylight.

The lifeboat returns to the scene

Islander Dr Addison was retired and suffered badly with rheumatoid arthritis. Nonetheless, he joined the island medical officer, Dr Ivers, aboard the lifeboat at first light the next day.

He recalled:

> *'A line was fired over him but he was washed off in trying to get hold of it so the lifeboat was taken in again and he was rescued.'*

'When day broke, three men were seen clinging to the rigging, and one man in the crow's nest who seemed to be dead.

'The lifeboat was taken close to the wreck and three lines were fired over the foremast.

'The first broke, the second fell short, the third was successful but the ship-wrecked men seemed unable to make use of it, and successively fell or were washed off into the sea finally to be picked up by the lifeboat which made three trips amongst the broken water and rocks for that purpose.

'A man was then seen on Scilly Rock itself, a line was fired over him but he was washed off in trying to get hold of it so the lifeboat was taken in again and he was rescued.'

Thirty-two saved, but six crewmen lost....

Two of the four men rescued were almost lifeless, but the doctors revived them as the lifeboat sped back to St Mary's. It then returned for a further, but fruitless, search.

Of the *Isabo*'s crew of 38 who had set out from Lussinpiccolo in Italy, 28 men were rescued by the Bryher boats and four by the lifeboat.

Of the six who were lost, one died in the rigging, but what exactly became of the others was never known.

One of the men rescued from the rigging by the lifeboat owed his life to Mrs Janey Slaughter who revived him with mouth-to-mouth resuscitation when he collapsed on St Mary's.

She then looked after him for three weeks. After spending that long awful night in the rigging, he was completely black-and-blue from exposure and bruising. Mrs Slaughter stated that when he was brought ashore she believed him to be an African.

Forty years later, Signor Rolli from Venice, by then in his sixties and a sea Captain, returned to thank Mrs Slaughter again for his life.

Janey Slaughter with Third Officer Rolli, on the left of the picture, in 1927.

Signor Rolli (centre) with rescuers Leonard Jenkins and Long John Jenkins in 1966, on board one of the original rescue boats at the scene of the wreck, for a BBC documentary.

The selflessness of islanders

The memory of the night that the *Isabo*
foundered stayed with Norman Jenkin's wife:

> *'I could hear from Bryher the men screaming in
> the water. When they were brought ashore we
> gave up our beds to them.*
>
> *'We couldn't understand them and they couldn't
> understand us. But we managed to feed them.
> They were Italians mostly, but there were some
> Estonians.'*

> ***'I could hear
> from Bryher
> the men
> screaming in
> the water.'***

Roll of Honour

The roll call of Bryher men, who all were heroes that night,
makes interesting reading:

The *Czar* Crew
*W E Jenkins, S Pender, W T Pender, F Jenkins, A T Jenkins, Rev
E R Pearce, N Jenkins and J J Jenkins.*

The *Sunbeam* Crew
*C Jenkins, E R Jenkins, S T Jenkins, J Jenkins, J E Pender and
S G Jenkins.*

The *Ivy* Crew
E Jenkins, S Jenkins and J S Jenkins.

Of 17 crewmen, all but one were named Pender or Jenkins.
Each was a father or son and a family breadwinner, and most
were related to one another.

Yet once again – as they always did – each selflessly put his life
at risk to save others; strangers who had been wrecked on the
cruel rocks of Scilly.

Italian heroes, too

There were also Italian heroes that night. The young 29-year-
old captain of the *Isabo* – gave a graphic description:

> *'Within 10 minutes of striking the rocks in the fog she
> started to break up. The men and I ripped off the
> hatches and threw them into the sea to act as rafts.*
>
> *'I went to the bridge, but the heavy seas drove me onto
> the upper bridge, and eventually swept me off. Many of
> us were swimming or clinging to wreckage and were
> rescued by the Bryher men.'*

Two men who never made it were the engineers who stayed at
their post in the bowels of the ship to try and keep power
going, and then drowned as the ship broke up.

Shipwreck! The *Isabo*

The story of the Mate

The 24-year-old mate was swept into the sea:

'I floated on an oar until I got to a rock. I swam around to find the lowest place to land and came to a place where the sea left the rock 15-ft exposed.

'I waited for a big sea to lift me over, then I struck in with it and came on top of the rock – still with my oar. As the sea went back I got a strong grip and crawled quickly up.

'I was naked; I walked round to find shelter and eventually found a little cave, and I spent the night massaging my body for warmth and sometimes going round the rock to try and find other floating men. I found none, and did not know all night of the other men being rescued nearby in the fog.'

> *'I was naked; I walked round to find shelter and eventually found a little cave, and I spent the night massaging my body for warmth...'*

The survivors from the Isabo *pose with some of their rescuers on St Mary's Quay*

The Major appeals for the retention of gigs

A blessing and thanks

Before leaving Scilly, the men stood bare-headed on the quay with arms extended in the Fascist salute, as their young captain blessed their dead comrades left behind, and thanked the locals for their hospitality and heroism.

Count Leon, a local Italian resident, echoed these sentiments and urged the men to be as good during their lives as they had been during and since the tragedy.

The Italians then filed aboard the *Riduna* for the trip to the mainland, shaking the hands of the islanders who crowded round to bid them farewell, then gave them three rousing cheers.

An avalanche of letters, cash awards and expressions of gratitude descended on Scilly from the Italian Government, the ship's owners and friends and relatives of the rescued.

The Italian Government struck 38 silver and bronze medals and issued vellum scrolls of thanks signed by Benito Mussolini.

RNLI medals and vellum thanks went to the St Mary's lifeboat crew, Dr Ivers, the *Czar* crew, the *Sunbeam* crew and the *Ivy* crew.

The awards were distributed at a Town Hall ceremony by the Major – Arthur Algernon – who made an impassioned appeal for the resurrection of the traditional Scillonian gigs.

'I earnestly appeal that gig crews be organised and the gigs be put in repair. They may not be as fast as motor boats but they are more reliable and they still have a part to play in the saving of life.'

The bravery of islanders

The *Czar*'s heroic efforts deeply affected the Church of England minister, the Rev Cyril Lancelot Thorrell-Barclay, and he resolved on practical action. He appealed to the Regatta Committee on St Mary's for a special gig race. To this day, the island men race their gigs every Friday night in the summer – including the *Czar*.

The Major's appeal was prescient. Twenty-eight years after the *Isabo* wreck, the gigs *Sussex* and *Czar* attended the wreck of the *Mando* in 1955 after she ran on to Golden Ball Ledge.

The wreck of the *Isabo* is just one of hundreds that dot the chart of Scilly. These wrecks live on in faded scrolls, in carefully preserved medals, in the memory of a few elderly islanders – and in the grand old gig, the *Czar*.

It was a night when two Bryher families sent out all their menfolk to rescue unknown souls drowning on the Scilly Rock. It wasn't the first time, and it wouldn't be the last.

A haunting impression of that night came from the Baptist minister, the Rev Pearce who rowed in the *Czar* with the Jenkins and Penders:

'The experience of being so close to men in grave danger yet unable to rescue them is a terrible one'.

For him, and for others on Scilly, the satisfaction of saving 32 sailors could never compensate for the sadness of losing six others to the sea.

Mussolini signed the vellum scrolls of thanks

'The experience of being so close to men in grave danger yet unable to rescue them is a terrible one.'

St Nicholas church contains a poignant memorial to the Dorrien Smith family's losses

The Fourteenth Chapter
*In which Arthur Algernon and
Eleanor suffer tragedy as
great as any family have had
to endure in war-time*

In 1936 Arthur Algernon posed for a photograph in the conservatory at the Abbey with his eldest son and heir, Robert who had just been commissioned as an officer in the 15th/19th Hussars.

hen Prime Minister Chamberlain announced that the country was at war with Germany on Friday, 1 September 1939, Arthur Algernon must have wondered how it would affect his country, his island and his family.

By then their eldest son Robert was 29 and a career Army officer with the 15th/19th King's Royal Hussars. Three years earlier he had married Rosemarie Lucas-Tooth.

Daughter Anne was 28 and single. Tom was 26 and a promising young naval officer.

Their other daughter Innis was 23 and living at home. Lionel was 21 and, after leaving Eton, had gone up to Oxford where, perhaps influenced by the early aviators on Tresco, he joined the university Air Squadron.

Francis was 18 and still at Eton. Young Helen was just seven.

The Second World War

The two grown-up Dorrien Smith daughters both joined the WAAF. Anne spent the war in Egypt as a photographic interpreter.

Innis remained in Britain for the whole war training WAAFs – the only one, apart from the child Helen, not posted abroad.

*Anne in
Cairo, 1942*

*Innis – home on
leave in 1944*

Robert was already in the Army and Tom was serving in destroyers as a lieutenant.

Lionel immediately left Oxford to join Cranwell to train as an RAFVR fighter pilot.

Francis left Eton shortly after war was declared and after a brief period working in a munitions factory in Scotland, got into uniform as quickly as he was allowed with the Rifle Brigade.

*Lionel and Francis at the
outbreak of war*

*Tom aged 24
in 1935*

Lionel left Cranwell as a pilot officer to join 79 Squadron, recently re-equipped with Hurricanes and based at Biggin Hill.

By May 1940 the German *blitzkreig* had rolled over the Low Countries and was pushing into France. In a desperate attempt to stop the Germans reaching the Channel and cutting off the British and French armies, 79 Squadron was sent to France and thrown against superior numbers of Luftwaffe aircraft. It was a disaster. The RAF lost 100 planes and 80 irreplaceable pilots.

*Lionel at
Cranwell
1939*

On 20 May, the British made a stand against Rommel's Panzers at Arras. With them was Robert and the 15th/19th Hussars.....

The deaths of three sons

January 1940 – Lionel, in his new pilot officer uniform, walks through the Abbey Garden with his mother on his way to war. Brother Francis wheels his suitcase in a wheelbarrow.

Tragedy

The war was just eight months old when tragedy hit in May 1940.

At the Abbey Arthur and Eleanor received the telegram. It told them that their son Lionel had taken off in his Hurricane on 20 May and was missing, believed killed, somewhere over France. His squadron had moved from Kent and flown to France. There they were thrown into the desperate battle to try to hold back the Germans who were advancing towards Dunkirk with the British army trapped between them and the sea.

On the ground, involved in the same battle outside Arras their eldest son Robert was fighting with the Hussars.

Within the hour Arthur and Eleanor received the second telegram bearing the almost unbelievable news that their eldest son Robert had died of his wounds on exactly the same day – 20 May.

It is impossible to imagine the grief and shock that must have engulfed them. But theirs was a tough generation who believed that to discipline emotion was a strength and an ingredient of leadership. Today, lesser men talk of the need for public emoting and personal counselling.

That day Arthur had arranged a meeting on the next-door island of Bryher. In the afternoon Arthur and Eleanor gathered up seven-year-old Helen and ordered the boatman to fetch the boat. They attended the meeting exactly as normal.

The war had not finished with the family.

Four years later, following the successful landings on D-Day in 1944, Allied troops fought their way into Normandy. With them was young Francis: 22 years old and a junior officer in the Rifle Brigade.

Just outside Bayeux a stray German shell landed right next to him. He was killed instantly along with three of his soldiers.

Arthur and Eleanor opened and read the telegram. Three of their four sons were now dead, killed on active service fighting Hitler's Third Reich.

Tom was still serving in the Navy and had been given his first command – *HMS Chiddingfold*. Anne was serving in Egypt, Innis was stationed in Britain and young Helen was still at home.

Avenge the *Hood*

On 24 May 1941, twelve months after the deaths of Lionel and Robert, the country was shaken by terrible news from the Denmark Straits.

The pride of the Royal Navy, *HMS Hood* engaged the German battleship *Bismark*. Within ten minutes the mighty *Hood* was sunk. All but three of her crew of 1,410 men died instantly as her magazines exploded.

Two years earlier, the *Hood* had been lying at anchor in the sunshine in St Mary's Roads.

HMS Hood *in St Mary's Roads before the war*

Tom Dorrien Smith was 'Number One' – the First Lieutenant – in *HMS Zulu*, one of a flotilla of Tribal class destroyers that joined the chase to avenge the *Hood*.

A Catalina flying-boat spotted *Bismark* 60 miles away and the flotilla steamed to meet her. The objective was to hold *Bismark* up long enough for the British battle fleet to arrive.

Each destroyer carried out a torpedo attack under heavy fire. *Zulu* released her torpedoes from just 3,000 yards, closer than any other ship came to *Bismark*.

With shrapnel flying round the bridge Tom was lucky to escape uninjured, the compass binnacle collecting some red-hot metal heading straight for his chest.

The torpedo attack was successful, *Bismark*'s steering gear was damaged and she was finally finished off by the cruiser *HMS Dorsetshire*.

HMS Zulu

Tom, while Commanding Officer of
HMS Chiddingfold *at the end of the war*

145

A Coastal Command reconnaissance photo showing Angele Rouge *alongside New Grimsby Quay before leaving on a mission*

The Fifteenth Chapter

*In which, 50 years after the
Second World War, the
incredible story of SOE's
Tresco operations is revealed*

*Charismatic leader – the Frenchman Daniel Lomenech
– photographed at sea on a mission to France in 1944*

**During the Second World War
top-secret missions from
Tresco helped change history.
High-speed launches disguised
as French fishing trawlers
crossed the Channel to ferry
agents and documents in and
out of Nazi-occupied Brittany.
Historians have said that their
achievements saved thousands
of lives in the D-Day landings.**

**In 1998 some of the men who
sailed in Tresco's 'Mystery
Boats' had their first reunion
back on Scilly. These are
their first-hand accounts of a
secret war waged by men
barely out of their teens.**

*In 1998 a display board
commemorating Special Forces
based on Tresco during the
Second World War was unveiled
at St Mary's Museum.*

*A group of 30 men and women,
all in their eighties, gathered in
the Museum. Most were British,
but there were also three well-
dressed Frenchmen and an
elderly French woman.*

*Later we walked down the street
to lunch at the Atlantic Hotel.
Over the meal, they talked of
their war...*

During the darkest days of the Second World War, when Hitler occupied France and Britain stood alone, a small team of young naval officers and other ranks, French and British, carried out a series of top-secret missions from Tresco.

Their story was only released under the 50-year secrecy rule; for many years our government was concerned that the operations that had been carried out from Tresco might one day need to be repeated should Europe ever be occupied again.

Listening to the gentle banter and quiet good humour one realised that in a world with so few real heroes that here were men of valour, dignity and chivalry. If Arthur and his Knights really were buried on Scilly then they must have silently dipped their lances to those old warriors that day.

Daniel Lomenech and a plan....

Lomenech photographed by the steps close to Braiden Rock in New Grimsby. They used them as a discreet embarkation point. A field telephone was concealed in the heather nearby so that they could inform headquarters when they were leaving.

In 1942, as young and untested boys, they sailed from Tresco in adapted French fishing boats across to Nazi-occupied Brittany. They retrieved agents, dropped off supplies and extracted the head of de Gaulle's biggest and best intelligence network in western and northern France. 'Remy' (Colonel Rénault) and his family were snatched from under the noses of the SS, together with top-secret German blue-prints of all the coastal defences between Cherbourg and Honfleur.

As a direct result of their recovery of the plans of the German defences a great many lives were saved in the later D-Day invasion of France.

As they reminisced, one name kept cropping up. Daniel Lomenech. He had been their inspiration and leader; a Frenchman who had escaped from occupied France and who had an extensive knowledge of the Breton fishing industry. The desire to see France free of the jack-boot burned deep within Lomenech.

He escaped to England from France at the third attempt in September 1940. By early November that year he re-entered France as an intelligence agent.

Briefly returning to England before Christmas 1940, he left again for France with three others, but was compromised and came back to England again for the third time, this time meeting a British submarine off the Brittany coast.

After this career as a secret agent in France he was assigned to a Royal Navy submarine in 1941 with the rank of Sub-Lieutenant RNVR. Their mission was to collect agents, passengers and mail off the Brittany coast from small French fishing boats. Lomenech although an old hand at the espionage game was still only 21 years old.

It was Lomenech who suggested replacing the submarine with a diesel-engined trawler operating from Tresco. The boat would blend in with the French fishing fleet and would allow a much more flexible schedule for the shore-based agents.

By early 1942, a 65-foot Breton trawler *Le Dinan* had been located in Newhaven where she had been acting as a patrol boat after fleeing occupied France. The Secret Intelligence Service (SIS) acquired her and refitted her.

Le Dinan *photographed off Tresco by Coastal Command in 1942*

Disguised as French trawlermen

The plan is tested....

Sub-Lieutenant Steven Mackenzie took command of *Le Dinan* with young Daniel Lomenech as First Lieutenant.

The rest of the crew were recruited from North Sea fishermen who were by then active service ratings in the Navy: 'Jasper' Lawn, Cookie Nash, Jock the Engineer. Dressed as French fishermen, they were the most incongruous of Special Forces.

They sailed from Dartmouth to Tresco to put on their 'war paint' in New Grimsby. Every time they went on a mission the grey trawler that passed as a patrol boat in British waters would be painted in the colours of a French fishing boat.

If anyone saw this transformation, the game would be up and the Germans might be alerted to the transfer of agents that was taking place right under their noses.

So in the secluded sound of New Grimsby, hidden from prying eyes, they changed from warship grey and the White Ensign to a blue hull, brown upperworks and a French name and number.

Steven Mackenzie on board Le Dinan

Left: *Coxswain 'Jasper' Lawn* ***Above***: *The crew of* Le Dinan *disguised as French fishermen*

To test the theory of passing themselves off as French trawlermen, they undertook two reconnaissance missions, on one occasion landing near Concarneau with impunity – right under the noses of the Germans.

Then in June, after once again painting the trawler in New Grimsby Sound, they sailed on a mission of supreme national importance....

Despite the informality of the Special Forces, both officers and men attended church parade at St Nicholas church

A mission of supreme importance

Le Dinan *photographed just off Tresco as she left for France*

The *Confrèrie Notre Dame* was the largest and most productive of the Free French intelligence networks operating in Occupied France. The creator and head of the organisation was code-named 'Remy' (Colonel Gilbert Rénault).

The Gestapo were closing in on him. He had to be extracted from France with his family as a matter of supreme urgency. If any of them were captured and tortured the whole intelligence network might be compromised.

Some idea of the danger that Remy faced can be gauged from this telling paragraph in his memoirs:

'I had sachets prepared for me in place of the usual pills of cyanide of potassium, the taking of which causes, it appears, extreme agony just before death.

'Morphia on the contrary would give me – should I need to use it – a gentle sleep from which I would never awake.'

This is how the Commanding Officer, Sub-Lieutenant Steven Mackenzie, described his trip after leaving Tresco:

'We had an escort of Beaufighters to protect us half-way across the Channel, three planes circling widely about the ship, relieved in relays from St Eval. Even so, we had three hours of unescorted daylight sailing to put us 20 miles from Ushant by the time darkness fell. At 10 pm our air escort left us, flying low and waggling their wings in farewell.

'This was the most dangerous part of the voyage crossing an area forbidden to fishing craft, and where a sighting by German air patrols would give the game away completely. We chugged on under a cloudless sky....

'By dawn we were south of Brest, the sea was like a mirror. At 10 in the morning we were among the crabbing fleet. As we sailed down the Baie-d'Audierne we could see the white villas shimmering in the sun. The lighthouse of Penmarc'h, the highest in the world, beckoned us on. Beyond it lay the Glenan Isles where our business called us.

'We reached our position with half an hour in hand. After an hour and a half nothing had appeared. Then at 6 o'clock in the evening black smoke appeared on the horizon, quickly followed by the appearance of five German corvettes. We held our course anxiously. Would they pass? Had Remy been caught and our plans uncovered?

'As the corvettes came on Jasper the coxswain nudged my arm and pointed to the islands. A tiny white sail had appeared. The excitement grew intense, the corvettes lent the final touch of colour to the situation. They passed us belching black smoke, the nearest less than a cable distant. We could see the captain examining us through glasses from the bridge, watched by German sailors on deck.

'We held our thumbs and turned our back on them. Then they were past, the casual inspection over.'

'We watched the white sail tacking to and fro until the corvettes had disappeared. We let it approach until we could identify it; everything fitted with the description we held. 30 feet long, single mast, green hull.... We made our signal, identified ourselves and went alongside.

'It seemed amazing that so many people could be concealed in that cockleshell of a boat. They had survived a German inspection when the vessel left harbour. Now they emerged. A woman first, then Mme Remy, then three children aged between 5 and 11, a man with several suitcases, and finally Remy himself – a parcel full of papers tied with string in one hand and a six-month baby in the other. They were helped on board, then the stores we had brought for the fishermen were handed over – petrol, oil, food and tobacco. In five minutes it was over, the warps were cast off.

'As she passed us to wave goodbye, the French skipper pointed to the sky. A patrolling Heinkel was approaching, but too far to have seen us together. We made gestures of contempt and then headed out to sea.

'We made an offing from the land and hove-to for the night. At dawn we began a slow cruise up the coast. Off the Ile-de-Seine an armed trawler came up from astern to pass close on the port side. As luck would have it, we were on top of a line of unattended nets; while she passed we stopped to haul them in, and were busy picking spider crabs from them when the officer of the watch swept us with his glasses from the bridge. A double triumph this, for Cookie had the crabs boiled in half an hour and we ate them on deck.

'The last and nastiest shock came at about ten in the evening. We were passing Brest, well to seaward, when we sighted three destroyers five miles to starboard. In a craft purporting to be an innocent French fisherman, we felt a little conspicuous as we made maximum speed northwards with dusk coming on.

'As though to confirm our worst fears, a destroyer broke away from the flotilla and headed towards us. For five minutes she held our course, gathering speed. We waited hopelessly for a challenge to blink from her lamp. Then she turned away and stopped. Exercise? We did not wait to see. The sky was growing darker every minute. We set about getting up the Lewis guns. From dawn onwards we would be in British waters, no longer in disguise, and allowed to hit back if necessary.

'At six the next morning, our air escort found us, and the children were allowed on deck for the first time. For 36 hours they and their mother had been shut up in the tiny wardroom cabin. They had not once complained.

'We did not make New Grimsby until three in the afternoon. The blue placid waters of the anchorage unfolded before us. White water boiled and tumbled on the rocks outside whilst within the water shimmered transparent and motionless. All was friendly, welcoming, unchanged. The place was deserted. But within half an hour we heard the drone of a motor gunboat's engines.

'Then around Shipman's Head she appeared, pennants fluttering green and white, bow-wave creaming the deep blue water, and from her loud-hailer came the martial crash of a Sousa march. She drew nearer, the music stopped and we could see the cheery faces on the bridge.

'The passengers were quickly transferred to the MGB and N51 was left to herself in the anchorage to resume the drab grey of an auxiliary naval trawler. How many times she changed colours later, I would not like to guess. But the link had been forged: it endured for more than two years!'

Remy, in beret, and his family were finally allowed up on deck once safely inside British waters

Remy never forgot the moment he arrived safely in New Grimsby harbour:

'We arrived at the Isles of Scilly. In a creek dominated by an old tower, our ship stopped, and tied up to a mooring. The water was wonderfully green and clear. The bottom which was at least eight metres under our hull, could be seen in the minutest detail. I could not resist the desire to dive in. I borrowed a pair of swimming trunks and jumped into the water which was as icy as it was beautiful.

'While I was swimming, I could hear a fanfare coming from the other side of the trawler. The children were calling me to come back on board, quickly, quickly.... I lost some time trying to find the rope ladder which hung down the hull and I missed the spectacle.

'Edith described it to me : a fast patrol boat of great beauty, long and white, shining in the sun, the crew standing to attention on the fore deck, all the flags flying, the sound of music (I learned later that it was a gramophone record played through a loud speaker) playing a military march, the officers on the bridge, standing to attention and saluting ... a truly royal reception.

'I felt I was completely out of place, in swimming trunks and dripping with water, amongst all these uniforms, and I hid myself.

'The patrol boat was an MGB (Motor Gun Boat) of large tonnage. We were made to go on board immediately and I dressed as fast as I could. We hardly had time to say our "goodbyes" to the officers of our dear trawler: Mackenzie, Lomenech, Townsend, the delightful crew, and then we were off again....'

The most valuable parcel of the war

Remy, clutching his parcel tied up with string, was in London within days.

The parcel was soon in Churchill's hands. It contained a Nazi blueprint of the Atlantic Wall, accurate to the very last gun emplacement and machine-gun nest. A large part of the planning for D-Day was based around this document. One military historian recently calculated its value to be worth perhaps a hundred thousand lives.

The plans had been stolen from the Gestapo by a professional house-painter and decorator from Normandy who went to SS headquarters in an attempt to get work. He deliberately quoted a ridiculously low price for the redecoration of the Caen headquarters of the German *Todt* organisation whose responsibility it was to build the defences of the Atlantic Wall. His offer was accepted.

> The parcel was soon in Churchill's hands. It contained a Nazi blueprint of the Atlantic Wall - accurate to the very last gun emplacement and machine-gun nest...

While undertaking his work, the house-painter picked the blue-prints off a desk and hid them behind a mirror in the room in which he was working, eventually removing them later.

Incredibly, the Germans took some time before they missed the plans – assuming that one of their own number had taken them. They never solved the mystery of where they had gone, and the *Todt* organisation, whose office it was, was afraid to draw attention to the loss which reflected badly on their security.

Engine problems on the Motor Gun Boat

But it was not all plain sailing after they left Tresco. Petty Officer Frank Rhodes described a trip that he made to Scilly in *MGB 318*:

'From our base in Dartmouth we were directed to Falmouth where we took aboard some 40-gallon drums of 87-Octane fuel which was to be transported to St Mary's on the Isles of Scilly. The Skipper and myself studied the maker's drawings to make sure that the drums were placed where there was adequate support below decks to prevent damage.... and away we went.

'Without mishap we arrived at the Quay at St Mary's where we found that the fuel was destined for a Belgian fishing vessel which was fitted with deck tanks and bore an alternative Royal Navy number in addition to its Fishing Boat details; either could be displayed. A Hall Scott engine had also been fitted. The crew spent ages transferring the fuel using a pump with two seats, one either side, and facing a pump handle whereby two operators could take turns to pump the fuel.

'Eventually, the fishing boat sailed and we were left to enjoy the relaxation of the Isles and the fresh dairy products, until some days later two RAF Beaufighters signalled that the fishing boat was returning. We went alongside to allow a passenger aboard, and he disappeared into the wardroom of 318.

'Immediately, we set sail for Falmouth and were cruising along nicely when Sparks reported severe interference on his radio. So I rigged the phones with long extension leads and shouted down the engine room hatch to isolate each bank of plugs in rotation (the routine for locating faulty plug leads).

'Suddenly everything stopped and I was flung into the engine room to find smoke rising from the port engine. The starter contacts on the engine had welded together. The motor continued to rotate, finally seized, and took out the main fuse which supplied all power on board. Fire appliances appeared as if by magic, and the fire was soon out and the starter removed.

'The Skipper was rather concerned as we had the VIP on board, but he soon relaxed when we got away on starboard and centre engines, and then started the port engine by trailing in the port engine clutch. The whole incident took less than it has taken me to describe, due to the superb fire-fighting training of Coastal Forces, and we made good time to Falmouth, and our passenger was placed on the train to London. I understand that he was picked up from a fishing boat somewhere off France.'

FRANK RHODES 2372

John Garnett as a rating before getting a commission as an officer.

An accidental hero

Another naval officer who spent his war in small boats with SIS was John Garnett, father of Virginia Bottomley, the former Conservative Secretary of State for Health. He wrote down many of his experiences:

'I joined the Navy after one year at Cambridge as a volunteer in September 1941. I was sent to Collingwood to train and then to the battleship *Malaya* as a Topman. We were a heavy escort to aircraft carriers flying Spitfires to Malta.

'Based at Gibraltar I finally got off at Freetown on the 4th July 1942 and came home to go to *King Alfred* for a commission.

'At the end of my time I was asked to volunteer for special service. I didn't know quite how to get out of it, and knew I couldn't face my mother if I did, so I accepted and found myself at an office then called NID(C), later called DDODI (Deputy Director Operations Division Intelligence).

An accidental hero   [cont]

'I was sent to join a French fishing boat – the *Président Henot* – then under overhaul at Shoreham.   I was the First Lieutenant to the commander, Lt Richard Townsend.   After overhauling our Deutz engine, converting the fish-hold to a wardroom and a creating an enlarged area down aft for the crew, we motored and sailed in convoy down to Falmouth. We broke down on a number of occasions mostly due to filters and arrived in Falmouth in early December.

'At once we prepared for an operation to the Jument Buoy south of the Glenans, but after painting into French colours, between Tresco and Bryher, the operation was aborted due to bad weather.   We returned after Christmas repainted again into French fishing boat colours and then set out from Tresco.

'We had on board wireless sets packed in tobacco sealed into French petrol drums.   We carried little armament, just bren guns, and we flew French flags as required by the Gestapo for boats fishing out of Concarneau.

tremendous dancing, and hugging and excitement at sea as they came alongside.

'We took on board a leading light of the French agents who brought over with him a rose tree planted in Lorraine earth for Madame de Gaulle, and a beautiful cigarette case bearing the Free French Cross of Lorraine, all made in France during the Occupation.

Garnett by the wheelhouse

'We then set out for home, and transferred the agents to a gunboat at Tresco, Having once again painted out all our French colours we put her back into grey and flying a White Ensign returned to Falmouth.'

John Garnett enjoying his breakfast during the mission

Everyone on lookout at our rendezvous point

"There was a French name and French numbers on each side of our sail and on the bow. We arrived off the Jument buoy and on the first day failed to make the rendezvous with the fishing boat coming out from Concarneau.

'But on the second day there she was, and we transferred our cargo to her and took on board two or three French agents. At the time of the transfer we wore our naval caps, I remember.

'We had in our crew one Breton sailor Raymonde Leroux who came from Penmarch, on the north-west corner of the Bay of Biscay. He knew the fishermen in the rendezvous boat and there was

Picking up an agent and off-loading supplies

An accidental hero   [cont]

The crew of MFV 2023. 'Cookie' Nash, Steven Mackenzie, Jasper Law, Daniel Lomenech and Joe Houghton

'The operation that I have described had been running for more than a year before I joined the In-Shore Flotilla.

'The leading light was Lt Daniel Lomenech who was a Frenchman, but carried a commission of Lt RN. He and Lt Richard Townsend had done a number of operations.

'Daniel was a man of enormous courage and the stories about him were legion. On one occasion when seeing a floating mine, he approached it and poked it with his boathook! He had carried out landings in the Glenans, burying post boxes in the sand; finally he had the good fortune to command the new boat specially designed and built for the work : MFV 2023.

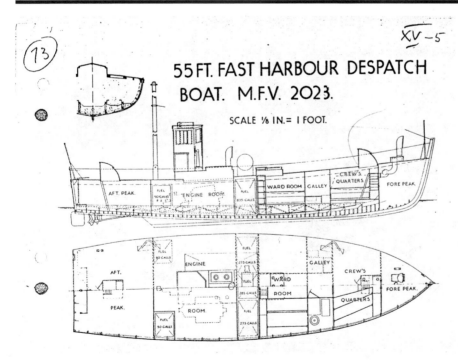

Laurent Giles' plans for the boat show a normal French fishing boat superstructure on a high-speed shallow draft hull.

The plans are discreetly headed 'Fast Harbour Despatch Boat'

Back in Britain, yacht designer Jack Laurent Giles started work in 1943 to design a high-speed hull with a French fishing-boat superstructure.

This would be the ultimate boat for the job, capable of a high-speed dash from Tresco under cover of darkness. Her speed would put her among the Breton fishing fleet by first light.

This top-secret vessel MFV 2023 was built at Cowes by Groves and Gutteridge. Inevitably it was young Daniel Lomenech who was given command. Sub-Lieutenant John Garnett became his second-in-command.

An accidental hero   [cont]

John Garnett continues his story...

'MFV 2023 was built at Groves and Gutteridge in Cowes and had the lines of a boat from Guilvanec. She was a 55-ft trawler but under water her draft was quite shallow, and in her fish hold she had two 500 hp Hall Scott engines.

'No longer was it necessary to go down to Scilly to change colour and then cross at 6 knots. She could go up into Frenchman's Creek in the Helford river and repaint there into her French colours. Then after dark she would motor slowly out until clear of British Radar range before turning on her Hall Scotts and crossing at 23 knots. She could appear to be fishing on the banks off the Glenans by dawn next morning. She could do the rendezvous and then travel back again through the next night.

'Thus instead of it being a 4 or 5-day operation from Scilly it became a 36-hour operation from Helford. Of course she had the speed; had she been intercepted she could have done something with it. If the other boats had been intercepted or challenged there was no way that they could have survived.

'There were always good stories surrounding Daniel Lomenech. For example, he had to take MFV 2023 back to Cowes for an engine overhaul when he was just finishing with the flotilla before re-joining submarines. They had to go in convoy because they were supposedly a 6-knot fishing boat.

'As they came up through the gate off Yarmouth on the Isle of Wight everybody formed up, as was proper, in naval seniority. The Hunt class destroyer went first, then came Daniel Lomenech as a Lieutenant RN in his little fishing boat. Behind came all the merchant ships and finally an armed trawler.

'Coming up to Cowes the Hunt class destroyer increased its speed because they wanted to give leave that evening. She went up to 12 knots, and the little fishing boat behind him went up 12 knots also. So she increased to 16 knots and the fishing boat did the same.

'Finally the Hunt went up to 20 knots and the fishing boat followed. The senior officer of the convoy on board the Hunt signalled to Daniel "What is your maximum speed?" He flashed back "You would be surprised", put her up to 28 knots, ran round the Hunt's bow and shot into Cowes.

"He had totally compromised the secret boat and there was talk about whether or not he should be court-martialled, but I expect as usual he got away with it!"

MFV 2023 at speed

> In wartime, with no lights, it was almost suicidal to attempt what they achieved.

The weather often prevented missions from taking place and added to the difficulties faced by the navigators. These individuals performed miracles in guiding the boats to the exact buoy or rock in Brittany that would be the rendezvous point.

The Brittany coast is one of the most dangerous in the world – even in perfect conditions but in wartime, with no lights, it was almost suicidal to attempt what they achieved.

David Birkin – father of actress Jane and married to actress Judy Campbell, whose husky voice made *A Nightingale Sang in Berkeley Square* so famous – was renowned for his ability to get any boat to any rendezvous in any weather. His efforts were even more remarkable since he suffered from chronic seasickness and wore thick glasses to correct bad eyesight. Without his intuitive skills few of the missions would have been successful. He proved that navigation could be an art as much as a science.

An accidental hero   [cont]

'Of course operations never went perfectly and there were many false starts. There were tremendous complications in getting messages back to Paris, down to agents in Concarneau, through HQ in London and the wireless communications centre at Bletchley – and finally down to us at Helford or to our scrambler telephone hidden in the heather at New Grimsby on Tresco.

'Having finally got a rendezvous time, then off we would go. The weather could be quite appalling, with force 8 or force 9 and on a couple of occasions we simply couldn't make it against the weather.

'Of course the fact was that with those wonderful sea boats, if the crew could survive then the boat certainly could – but it could be a real battle.

'On one occasion the weather had been quite dreadful. The rendezvous was made and we were coming back out around Penmarch in order to head back up to Scilly passing 30 miles off Ushant. As we finally weathered Penmarch we hit something under water. We didn't blow up but we lost a blade off the propeller and we didn't think we could run the engine.

'So we set our sails, but we weren't going to weather Ushant. We then tried the engine and there was a lot of vibration and leaking oil. Keeping her tighter than close-hauled we managed to edge up round Ushant but we couldn't go on heading for Scilly. We then paid off and ran away down to Dartmouth and managed to get her in like that.

'On another occasion, coming back with agents from a successful operation, we thought all was going well but you always paid for it. At about 2300 we were crossing the neck of Brest coming up to Ushant about 30 miles off shore. Suddenly, just before the change of watch, a huge searchlight picked us out. We were bathed in light and we thought "My God, a destroyer has got us at last!"

"We didn't know what it was, as we didn't know then about Lee Light Wellingtons who picked up German submarines on the surface with their radar and then dived and dropped their depth charges. On this occasion God was kind to us and the pilot must have looked first and seen that it was a fishing boat and not a submarine. He didn't drop depth charges around us. The coxswain on watch never really recovered from that appalling experience!'

Sir Brooks Richards served with SOE during the Second World War and his book *Secret Flotillas* documents the Special Forces operations from Tresco in which he took part, as well as other activities in Northern France, North Africa and Italy.

It was Sir Brooks who arranged the reunion and the presentation on St Mary's that I attended. I am grateful for his permission to reprint the accounts above and some of the photographs.

Sir Brooks Richards photographed in 2002 at a Special Forces reunion in Brittany

Paul O'Brien's story

Another young RNVR sub-lieutenant with Special Forces on Tresco was Paul O'Brien. These are his recollections of serving on MFV 2023 which had been given the French name *Angele Rouge.*

'This photograph shows the crew of *Angele Rouge* – our secret high-speed launch designed by Laurent Giles to look like a French fishing boat.

'Both this photo and one of myself were snapped by JJ Tremayne just before we set off on an operation in mid-September. Note the dummy wooden 'gallows'....

'I mention the 'gallows' because it was on this trip that we were nearly rumbled.

'We were on our way home with two agents, and were off the Raz du Seine on a day of intense heat and unimaginable glassy calm when every sound seemed to carry for miles. We were meandering along at a couple of knots, purportedly fishing, but our net and trawl doors were just two buckets slung from said 'gallows'.

'To the agents' disgust, and ours, a convoy of two submarines and several escorting heavy patrol boats – rather like scaled-down destroyers – appeared dead ahead and steamed quite meaningfully towards us.

Le Dinan photographed in French Colours in Tresco Channel

Paul O'Brien's story   [cont]

'As we were trawling, to have altered course more than a little would have been a give-away to an alert observer, so we had to grin and bear it as they closed on us and passed no more than 200 yards off our starboard beam.

'A few minutes before this, there was a goose-pimply moment which pricked the euphoria of the agents we had just recovered. A flight of Junkers-88s swooped over us and released some shiny objects! Recognition signals for the subs, I hoped. So they proved, but the agents thought otherwise and dived under the nets secured along the gunwales. JJ advised them to stay there!

'As the ships passed, they were so close that we could see the faces of the crew, leaning over the rails, listening to some lugubrious German love-song. I was observing all this from the forrard hatch, partly hidden by the coaming. Good, I thought, they can't leave the convoy to ask us for some fish – always a big worry because *Angele Rouge*'s buckets were a dead loss. This time, though, we had bought a deckload of fish from Newlyn, stowed in ice.

'Just then, JJ in the wheelhouse suddenly put *Angele Rouge* hard astern. There were literally clouds of smoke from the Hall-Scott's carefully hidden exhausts – not to mention churned-up white water and spray! Surely, I thought, this is curtains. They can't ignore that. But they did. They must have had a good lunch.

'It turned out that JJ had spotted, just in time, a large Seine net only 50 yards ahead – and he had to keep our twin props clear of that, or else!

'Ever so slowly, it seemed, the convoy drew away and a few hours later in the fading light we were on our way at a rate of knots.

'The agents were still aggrieved. They had expected us to run for it – which would have been fatal. But JJ had done the right thing, and we were there to prove it.

'When some years later he gave me the photo no wonder he had written on the back "Wot, no fish?"'

Back in the Helford river, John Garnett was in continuous practice with specially made surf-boats. These were necessary for landing and retrieving people and stores in the rough waves off the Brittany beaches. He soon became an expert.

Meanwhile, a magnificent private yacht had been requisitioned to serve as headquarters for the Special Forces in the Helford river.

An accidental hero   [cont]

'One of the great moments was the coming of Lord Runciman's yacht *Sunbeam 2*, a three-masted schooner that was used as the In-Shore Flotilla's headquarters. Later she dragged her moorings, her buoys bumping all the time under her stern. Lt Commander Nigel Warrington Smyth swung her around on the tide and took her down river, whilst they moved the buoys further out and then we came back up again and moored up fore and aft.

'At the time I was under great pressure from my new wife not to spend the evening helping but to come ashore. However I thought it was my duty to play my part in this operation with Nigel.

'As it turned out later, sitting on his desk on board *Sunbeam,* was a recommendation for me to have accelerated promotion to Lieutenant. He had decided that if I stayed on board he would sign it and if I didn't he wouldn't.

'So although my wife Barbara was simply furious, later on she quite liked my second shining RNVR stripe.'

An accidental hero [cont]

'I've talked about heavy weather, but of course there was also the problem of thick weather. On one occasion we left the Bishop light going south for the rendezvous and went way out as always around Ushant then made our landfall on the great lighthouse at Eckmul on Penmarch at the top of the Bay of Biscay before turning in under Brittany and coming in on the Jument buoy. Richard Townsend was in command. It was terribly thick and we could not see the lighthouse. Visibility must have been down to a quarter of a mile at the most.

'As we came in we could hear the lighthouse booming and we could hear water breaking on rocks. We continued to creep in when suddenly out of the fog in front of us came a great seamark. We immediately turned about to steam out and ran straight into a German convoy that was coming round Penmarch with a German naval escort. To Richard's eternal credit instead of turning back into the rocks and away from the convoy, as no French fishing boat would have done, he came straight out through the middle of the convoy, holding his course and speed.

'We kept Raymond Laroux on deck, and I was on deck as well. As we pretended to be washing down we were watched from the bridge of the German destroyer. The captain's binoculars stared at us, watching us. We just kept on with our affairs and went through the convoy and out into the fog again.

'There were two parts of the intelligence organisation working on the Continent. One was the secret service SIS – MI6 – that dealt with intelligence and in the end belonged to the Foreign Office, and was represented by Anthony Eden at the Cabinet table. The other was sabotage – SOE – that belonged to the Ministry of Economic Warfare and was represented by Hugh Dalton. These two organisations were utterly split from top to bottom, right down to even the most local level.

'In order to patch things up in the Helford River, they cleverly put Nigel Warrington Smyth, who grew up as a boy on the river, in charge of SIS and based him on board *Sunbeam 2*. Ashore was SOE under Lt Commander Bevil Warrington Smyth, his elder brother. Finally, in order to make certain that the brothers always got on they put in charge of the whole Helford base Lt Warrington Smyth, the Local Naval Officer (LNO), who was their father!

'On the whole although many plans were made, in the years that I was there SOE did nothing very much as far as I could discover other than practice and prepare boats. They were thoroughly cooperative and helpful but didn't do much out on the river.

'They had, however, an extraordinarily jolly young man called John Wilkinson, fair-haired and the son of the man who was the managing director of the Power Boat Company before the war. He was in charge of HSL (high speed launch) 115 that had belonged to the RAF and had been used for air sea rescue and could do 47 knots.

'John Wilkinson like many of the rest of us, loved a Wren called Elaine Pilgrim. Her parents ran the Nansidwell Hotel, but as far as we knew nobody had ever made much headway with Elaine. She used to come to dances wearing a blue skirt with rings round it, and John Wilkinson was determined to have a close relationship with Elaine. So he let it be known to her that he was about to go on a most secret and difficult operation from which he might never come back. In the previous week he told her that he was to go on Tuesday night and that it was very stressful and worrying, and he was saddened that their relationship might come to an end because he would be lost.

'Finally on the Monday night when saying good-bye to her, he said that he expected to be back by 11 pm the next night and if he was not back by 1 am then things were very bad, and if not back by 2 am then it was all over.

'The following night, he never went to sea at all. He didn't ring her at 11 pm, 1 am or at 2 am, but waited until 2.30 am before ringing her up and saying that he was back safely. At which, of course, she tumbled into his arms!

'Whether this story is true or not I have no idea, but we all heard about it and thought that John Wilkinson was a bit of a lad. Elaine Pilgrim remained a simply lovely lady.

'This story concerns Christmas 1943. The work of running agents by boat to Brittany was partly done by fishing boats out of the Helford River, but was also done by two gunboats based on Dartmouth under the command of Commander Davies. Occasionally they borrowed other MGBs and crews from coastal forces.

'In November 1943 a gunboat had gone across to the north-west edge of Brittany and had landed two surf boats – 14-ft long with beautifully made overhanging bows to ride the surf. The weather was so bad that they were unable to get back to

An accidental hero   [cont]

the gunboat. So the boats were taken ashore again, filled with stones and weren't discovered by the Germans. The crews were taken care of by our French agents over there.

'In the right moon period in December in the week before Christmas another gunboat went over to try to pick up the original crew together with all the people who had been there the previous month plus new people that had arrived to be taken off. The weather was so bad that the operation again failed. The boats' crews were totally exhausted, and there was nobody to man them for another immediate operation.

'On Christmas Eve, at dinner on board *Sunbeam*, I was called out to see Nigel Warrington Smyth, the commanding officer, who said that we were to provide the boat's crews for an operation on the following night: the night of Christmas Day. In order to do that, because the numbers waiting were now so great – there were more than 30 men on the beach – we would tow across the large SN6 – a 25-ft surf boat. I was to be responsible for the tow and for getting the boat there behind the gunboat as I was very keen on that kind of operation.

'The following day on Christmas morning I went in to Falmouth to get the charts and at 3 pm we towed down river with the surf boat behind the SOE seaplane tender 360, and out to meet the gun boat MGB 313 that had come round from Falmouth. We made her fast with a grass rope, with plenty of stretch and a wire as well and I sat aft on the gunboat all the way to France and towed her surfing on the stern wave of the gunboat. If of course she had got too far astern she would have swamped immediately, but if she could surf on the top of that wave then we could tow her at 26 knots all the way to France – 90 miles from the Lizard.

'Navigation was an amazing operation by the gunboat's crew. We were going into L'Aberwrach which is hard enough to get into through the rocks in peacetime with lights; and we were attempting it without any lights at all. The gunboat used an RAF direction-finding system where radio beacons gave a cross reference.

'The navigating officer brought us right up on the buoy, unlit, at the entrance to the channel. We then threaded our way up the estuary; on silenced engines, anchored, and a boat's crew with Howard Rendle as coxswain and six SOE oarsmen went ashore to Ile-Tariec which lay eight hundred yards from the gunboat anchorage. They

had to make two journeys and brought off 32 people.

'Very quietly we turned and left for home. However, no sooner had we got 20 miles off than the gunboat's engine broke down and there was a good deal of worrying about whether the engines would get started again before dawn, but they did, and home we came.

'As was usual, the agents coming out of France gave the naval officers scent that had come out from Paris three days before, when I got back to Helford I went ashore at eight in the morning and, it being Christmas, my wife was living in a house on shore. I woke her up and was able to give her, as a Boxing Day morning present: a bottle of Chanel. When her sister saw this bottle of Chanel on her dressing table, a week later, she said to her "Now I know what John's doing in the navy".

'Amongst the people we brought off there was an extraordinary faceless kind of man who might be anybody, and therefore you can't remember him. He brought ashore a roll of maps under his arm on which were plotted all the flying bomb sites right back to Holland. He had come across France, picking them up as he went and we brought him off in the extreme west.

'We also had a number of airmen on board. We had one in particular who had been flying in a Liberator which he thought was over Plymouth when he was suddenly shot out of the sky. He parachuted to the ground, ran to a road, stopped the first car and said "I am trying to get to Plymouth". The person replied "You're in France, you are near Brest, but you are in luck – get in".

'He took him back into Brest for the day and that evening, since he was an agent, brought him to be met by the gunboat. When he finally got back to London the next day he arrived only a day after he would have arrived had he landed north of Plymouth, instead of landing north of Brest.

'Among the 32 people we took off there were also a number of American airmen. They had crashed over France, and as always gathered in Paris where people were hidden much better that out in the countryside. They had somehow to be got back to England.

'They decided that since none of them spoke French the only way to handle this was to produce forged papers for the evacuation of a Deaf-and-Dumb Institution to the north-west of France.

An accidental hero [cont]

'False papers were made and they left the Paris station and came down to Brittany. They were unable to speak, and because of the shooting up and bombing of trains by the British, there were terrible delays and hold-ups and they went from village station to village station.

'The train got fuller and fuller. They were sitting on the floor and at one stage a woman got in with a pig in her arms and she let the pig slip and it fell onto an American airman's head and he immediately retorted "For God's sake, woman, take that damn pig off my head!".

'There was a terrible silence, as they were meant to be deaf-and-dumb and clearly here was an American right among them. Nobody said anything, nobody tipped anybody off, and they came on through to a little station just outside Brest where they were brought across to join the MGB.

'This story is concerned with the time of the invasion. D-Day was on Tuesday 6th of June and of course we saw the loading from the river; we had seen the roads widened leading to Trebah beach on the Helford River in order to cope with the transport to American tank landing ships. We just lay in the river waiting for orders.

'On the Thursday, D+2, we were told to leave at once for Portsmouth in one of the fishing boats, MFV 2028, *L'Oeure*. I was to be the First Lieutenant on this occasion. We went up by convoy, got there during Friday and waited for orders. The orders were to join the convoy, on Friday evening, for the beachhead JUNO at Courseulles.

'That night we carried out members of SIS, the people we worked for, to reconnoitre the ground in order to be ready to pass agents backwards and forwards through the beachhead and the front line. We were to be the forward base. We anchored off Seaview, Isle of Wight – my own home – and I was able to look ashore to where I had spent every holiday of my life, where my grandmother was living, and where my parents had built a house.

'We set out that night for area Z, known as Piccadilly Circus, where all the ships came in from all the ports of the south coast. There was tremendous activity in the centre of this vast area – south of St Catherine's and 10 miles across.

'The ships went out on the swept lanes to whichever part of the beachhead they were going.

We were on our way to Juno at Courseulles to get behind the 'Gooseberry', the sunk ships which protected the beach. We arrived there on the Saturday morning and unloaded our ZEEP, the water-going Jeep, and contact was made by the headquarters people with the Commodore ashore.

'Of all the extraordinary things.... on the Sunday, D+5, we were invited to lunch at the Lion d'Or, the lovely hotel in Bayeux. There we were sitting with French agents having lunch and paying in Francs printed in London. The previous Sunday they were trading with Nazi German Officers, paying, no doubt, in Francs printed in Berlin.

'When later we went back to the Lion d'Or, many years after, we discovered it wasn't a matter of just a week's difference. The front line had gone through Bayeux on the Wednesday. They were feeding German officers on the Tuesday, and feeding British Officers on the Thursday. So, in fact, the French missed only one day's trading!

'After five days on the beachhead we returned to Portsmouth to take another fishing boat back to lie over there to act as the reception area, for agents coming by MGB. We landed them and took them ashore, and we continued for two months with a boat over there taking it in turns. I was there for the vast bombing of Caen, with the whole sky filled with 4-engined bombers.

'I was also there for the terrible gales on D+12, when the worst northerly gales that had ever struck in recorded history blew down on us. We really wondered whether or not God was on our side. We in the fishing boat played a great part bailing ships out and helping with tremendous enthusiasm whenever seamanship was needed.

'There was a great moment when we were on the beach and things were very bad indeed. No ammunition had come ashore for at least two days. At that moment, who should come along the beach but a small man with a beret with two staff officers round him – and there was General Montgomery himself.

'What that did for the morale of people on that beach was simply staggering. Up to then, as a sailor, I had always thought that Montgomery was a bit of a bull-shitter. But there he was down there with us and we knew from then onwards it was going to be alright. He wasn't back somewhere, he was right up where the front line was.

An accidental hero   [cont]

'As the line advanced we moved our base forward. We spent some time on the English side at Shoreham and we also got a house in Dieppe. We then moved again with a base at Folkestone, running MGBs across to a house we had in Boulogne. At that point the operations involving the crews of the fishing boats from Helford came to an end, except for one crew of which I was the commanding officer. I was helped by a lovely New Zealander called Sub-Lt Norman Ettlinger.

'We were told to man a beautiful Danish-type fishing vessel that had been built specifically for landing agents and sabotage materials on the Danish coast. Our job was to lie alongside at Dover and then to go over to Ostend and on to Rotterdam to carry stores for the agents in Belgium and Holland to reward them for what they had done for the Allies.

'In fact what they wanted was not money, which was relatively useless during inflation times, nor cigarettes, but bicycle tyres. So once every fortnight we sailed with our decks filled with bicycle tyres from Dover. This was an exceedingly happy time; based at Dover, then the coast near Ostend and then on to Rotterdam where we made fast to the tram-lines because the whole of the edge of the docks had been blasted to pieces.

'It was when we were back in Dover at 8 o'clock in the morning in the little wardroom that I heard on the news that the war in Europe was over – VE day. I can remember bursting into floods of tears of relief and being quite unable to stop myself.

'That night my wife Barbara was down in Dover as it was a school holiday, and we went to Canterbury to spend the evening of VE Day, and for the first time for six years the cathedral was floodlit. This was an amazing end to the operations.

'In due course I went back to Helford to take *Sirene* round to Hayle for decommissioning and then later took 2032 back to the top of the Hamble to pay her off.'

John Garnett finishes his story with an epilogue....

EPILOGUE

'I went back to Cambridge to finish my degree; and then joined ICI as a clerk in Glasgow and worked my way up. In 1960 Barbara and I went for a week's holiday to Brittany in order to try to find *Sirene*. We searched Domannes and various other fishing ports and finally on our last day in Brittany we came to Cameret. I walked up on the sea wall side, and Barbara was walking on the beach, At the same moment we came round and there *Sirene* was – lying on her side.

'We heard that she was to be destroyed that Christmas and burnt because she was no longer of any use. We discovered the woman who owned her and went to meet her in a café. She spoke mostly in Breton; we spoke in rather stumbling French.

'She told us how *Sirene* had gone out fishing and then disappeared and gone off to the 'gueru'. She had been returned to them after the war but she had been altered about a lot. I asked if I could take off *Sirene* some of the carvings that the sailors had done.'

An accidental hero   [cont]

EPILOGUE

'There was a lovely little crest and a lot of iron work which was all going to be wasted and she said that I could. I went off to buy a hacksaw. We spent the afternoon cutting her main blocks off together with a whole lot of her ironwork and the little crests.   We put these in the back of our Thames van and in due course came out through Customs at Dover.

'I was very keen on listing everything I possessed for the Customs. When the officer read all this stuff, he said he didn't understand what all this was, could I show it him? I opened up the back door of the van. There was all this ironwork and he turned to me and said "There's no duty on junk." I said "It may be junk to you – it was our life's blood to us."

'The crest is in our boathouse in the Isle of Wight and the iron work has all been concreted into mooring stones and so the dinghies lie with their chains fixed to *Sirene's* metalwork. Her main sheet blocks are still used when there is a massive pulling operation to be done using a lot of children and grandchildren.   In between times they hold the boathouse doors open.

'In 1992 at half-term, we took the young girls of my second family, with my wife Julia to Bayeux and on the Friday we saw the tapestry of how the Normans invaded this country.

'The following day we went down onto JUNO beach at Courseulles, and saw where I had come ashore as part of those who had brought freedom to Europe to get rid of the ghastly Nazis, their cruelty to the Jews and all Europe. We stayed at the Lion d'Or, and there were many reminiscences, by them, and by me of 1944.

'On that second evening we went to a cemetery to show the 10-year old and the 7-year old something of what it was about. There we read on one of the stones:

> *'Gaily he came, gallantly he left me,*
> *But I have his son, a small sweet part*
> *of him.'*

'Charity, the 10-year old, wrote in the cemetery book. "We must never let this happen again, we must make a better world."

'Since then I have been re-inspired by the thought that he died to produce a better world. We are lucky enough to have lived to make a better world.

'That is what we must continue to do....'

Unveiling a Tresco memorial

And so on that lovely sunny afternoon on St Mary's I left the Atlantic Hotel and walked with Sir Brooks Richards to the Quay to catch a boat back to Tresco.

He asked me whether it would be possible to erect a small plaque on Tresco commemorating the exploits of the Special Forces in the Second World War.

A year later a small and distinguished party of 30 or so people gathered once again on Scilly to unveil the plaque that was placed on a rock overlooking New Grimsby Harbour.

This anchorage of New Grimsby Sound

served as a base for a secret naval flotilla from April 1942 to October 1943. British vessels, disguised as French fishing boats, penetrated deep into enemy waters off the Brittany coast to contact the **'Confrèrie-Nôtre-Dame,'** the most productive of the intelligence networks in German-occupied France.

In this secluded channel, the vessels exchanged their grey naval paintwork for the characteristic brilliant colours of South Breton fishing boats, taking care to avoid a freshly-painted appearance.

This sea-line of communications was devised by **Daniel Lomenech**, a 21-year-old Breton intelligence agent with excellent knowledge of the south Breton fishing industry. In June 1942 **Colonel Rénault**, head of the Confrèrie and his family, who were in extreme danger, were rescued in the vessel N51 'Le Dinan'. This expedition, commanded by **Lt. Steven MacKenzie RNVR** with **S/Lts. Richard Townsend RNVR** and **Daniel Lomenech RNVR**, also brought back a detailed plan of the coastal defences that the Germans were constructing along the Normandy coast. This information became the basis of the **D-Day Landings** of 1944 and ensured minimal loss of men and materials in that operation.

Holdsworth Special Forces Trust   2 July 2000

N51 Le Dinan

Daniel Lomenech

Sir Brooks and Lady Richards at the rock in New Grimsby where the plaque was fixed

This was the anchorage where the *Angele Rouge* and other boats lay before painting themselves as French trawlers and setting off under cover of darkness for Nazi-occupied France.

The unveiling party included General Sir Michael Rose, former head of the SAS, and also the Director of the Imperial War Museum. We stood with the few old warriors who were left.

Daniel Lomenech's son, watched by his mother, pulled away the tricolour from the plaque.

Just below us, Paul O'Brien, a survivor of many of those Special Forces missions, stood in a rowing boat and addressed us....

This is what Paul O'Brien said on that early evening of 2 July 2000 as we stood by the plaque overlooking New Grimsby harbour:

'Dear Friends and Scillonians

'This is a great day – and a memorable moment – for the families of the officers and crews of N51, A04 and 2023 *Angèle Rouge*. It is thus a great joy to have with us Ninon Lomenech and Ursula Townsend and their families.

'Sadly, Julia Garnett and Jean-Jacques Tremayne could not join us, but I do know that they are very proud of John and Jean-Jacques.

'JJ was Commanding Officer of 2023 for several operations. He was a very brave man and a splendid seaman – and I commend him to you.

'Of course, the many missions would not have been possible without our marvellous crews. They were nearly all fishermen, and they were not only sea salts, but the salt of the earth as well. You could not fault any of them.

'I know that both Daniel (Lomenech) and Richard (Townsend) would like me to remember and savour especially Jasper Lawn, Ralph Hockney (their two Coxswains) and Cookie Nash who kept us all alive with his amazing meals, come hell or high water.

'If we could not have managed without these men, nor could we have coped without our back-up team, of whom, first of all, was Captain Frank Slocum, DDODI, a Director of the SIS. His brilliant staff officer and immaculate planner Steven Mackenzie, and Nigel Warrington Smyth, Senior Officer Inshore Patrol. This was our nom de plume – or nom de guerre – and he kept us hard at it, as well as at our other activities.

'Our dear late friend Captain Tommy Tucker of the Royal Corps of Signals was our radio king who fitted us out with some remarkable radio equipment, and among many unheralded people serving on *Sunbeam 2* in Helford was the Wireless Officer, David Herbert, who kept watch for us with unswerving commitment.

'If Braiden Rock marked our departure, it was also our point of return to the genuine warmth, hospitality and kindness of the people of Tresco. Above all, we would like to thank and salute them for keeping "mum" for so long, and so successfully!

'I know the crews would have liked me to mention without fail John Williams of the New Inn and his wife who did so much to sustain their morale!

'Thus the plaque I will now unveil – it is not only for the ships, but will be a lasting memento and symbol of the continuing bond between us, our friends here, and all Scillonians.'

Vive La France!
Vive les Bretons!
Vive la Grand Bretagne!

The plaque at Braiden Rock

Later we all dined in a private room at the Island Hotel on Tresco. It was quiet, but full of thoughtful conversation and good company.

During the course of the evening, General Sir Michael Rose – himself a member of the Special Forces, former head of the SAS and commander of Allied Forces in Bosnia – made a comment that I have never forgotten. 'What these men did, and the plans that they were able to retrieve and bring back to Tresco probably saved a hundred thousand lives in the D-Day landings.'

It was an honour to have been part of the commemoration, to have been among heroes and to have learned something of the secret war of which Tresco was part more than 60 years ago.

The plaque that we unveiled at Braiden Rock is a short walk from the old Quay shop in New Grimsby. Take the cliff path along the harbour that starts behind the shop. After 200 yards you are faced by a steep outcrop of rock. To your left is a short path down to the sea. At the bottom – about 30 yards – is a worn set of steps from which they embarked.

On the rock next to the steps is the plaque. It's quite a private place, and you have to work a little to find it – but that, I think, is as it should be....

You can read much more detail and more first-hand accounts of the secret sea-line to Occupied France in Sir Brooks Richards' own history of Special Forces, *Secret Flotillas*.

While researching this story I came across an anomaly: Special Forces officers on Tresco frequently appeared in photographs under different names.

One in particular, 'JJ' or Jean-Jacques Tremayne also appears as J-J Allen. I queried this with Sir Brooks Richards. This was his reply:

'The picture of *Angele Rouge* – MFV2023 – showing the tricolour on the ship's bows were taken in New Grimsby on her return from an operation with J-J Allen in command. He's the small fellow looking over the bulwarks.

'He is also the chap in civilian clothes in the group of officers which includes Lord David Herbert and Nigel Warrington Smyth (partly effaced for security). The picture of the ship taken from the air shows her at speed during an operation.'

'The designer of 2023 was Jack Laurent Giles, then working in the Director of Naval Construction Office in Bath.

'J-J Allen and Jean-Jacques Tremayne are one and the same person. French Naval Officers who joined the Royal Navy after the Fall of France were in double jeopardy. Like de Gaulle himself, they might be condemned to death *in absentia* by court martial in France, but they were also violently disliked by the Gaullists who considered that all patriotic Frenchmen ought to join the Free French Forces. Hence their adoption of British pseudonyms.

'J-J's original surname was Gilbert, but presumably, after his stay in Cornwall, he preferred to adopt "Tremayne" rather than the "Allen" given him by the RN in 1940 when he became one of the officers in *Fidelity*.

'He was one of the very few survivors when that ship was lost with over 400 crew.'

Perhaps the last word in this curious and hitherto secret chapter of naval history, of which Tresco was part, belongs to 'Remy' – the head of their French Resistance in Brittany who was rescued with his family by Special Forces from Tresco.

Their trip to Tresco was not without tragedy. One of the two Beaufighters that had escorted them into British waters crashed with the loss of both the crew while flying low over the boat.

'I have saved this piece of paper, torn from a pad headed 'Naval Message', scribbled in pencil with all the mistakes – so moving when one thinks of the friendship which unites pilots.

'I thought of those two lads, very young, (I have since learned that they were brothers) setting out this morning on what they thought was a pleasure trip, and who had undoubtedly wished to entertain my children with their aerobatics, and who had met their death under a clear sky which merged with the calm blue sea. I have also saved three pieces of aluminium, which had broken off from the undercarriage when it was hoisted on to the deck.

'A friend in France being tortured to make him give away the secret of the place where I had hidden my family; two airmen abruptly snatched from life when they had come to protect us; and our young friend de Beaufort (Leger) who had accompanied us at the start of our adventurous voyage by taking us in his vehicle, and who was shot by the Germans on the very eve of the Liberation.

'When my children are much older, I will explain to them what their own lives are worth and how much had been paid for them, the debts they owe to all those people to justify so many sacrifices.'

Jean-Claude Rénault, son of 'Remy', at a commemoration in Brittany, 2002

Other events on Scilly during the war

The airport at St Mary's was first used in July 1939 with a mail and passenger service using Dragon Rapides. Before that, the planes had used the golf course. By the time that the service was terminated at the start of the war more than 10,000 passengers had used it. During the war, a mail service was reinstated.

On 3 June 1941, a Rapide was shot down by a Heinkel 111 returning from an abortive raid on the carrier *HMS Indomitable* at Barrow-in-Furness. Five members of the same family lost their lives. Six Hurricanes of 87 Squadron had been withdrawn only days earlier to be re-equipped.

Various aircraft made unscheduled visits with battle damage including a Whitley bomber, a Liberator of Coastal Command, various Sunderland flying-boats, a Catalina, a USAF C-47 and a P-38 Lightning. Walrus flying boats were also stationed on Scilly in a Search and Rescue role.

The RAF on St Mary's tallied six confirmed 'kills' and two 'probables'. Eight local aircraft were either lost or damaged.

The frigate HMS Nereus, *alongside for repairs in St Mary's after striking rocks*

The Wreck of U-Boat U-681

In 1998, divers located the wreck of German submarine U-681 near the Bishop Rock. She was built at Hamburg in 1944 (67.1 metres overall, 1,070 tons) and she belonged to 11 Flotille, a Frontflotille (Combat Flotilla) based in Norway.

Her commander, Werner Gebauer, struck a rock while submerged in

Broad Sound on 10 March 1945. Unable to stay underwater, U-681 attempted a surface passage to a neutral port in Ireland. But she was sunk the next day at 0930 by a Liberator bomber of VPB-103 Squadron, 7th Fleet Air Wing US Navy, based at Dunkeswell, Devon. Eleven of the crew of U-681 were killed and 38 survivors captured.

The BBC's Ralph Whitlock presenting the prizes at the Tresco show

The Sixteenth Chapter
In which the island recovers its community spirit after the Second World War

After the war, families across the country were reunited. The price of victory had been heavy and the country entered a period of austerity and rationing.

On Tresco the Major encouraged islanders to take part in agricultural shows and fetes that proved very popular.

Tresco's annual Agricultural Show was open not just to Tresco islanders but also to residents on other islands. Everyone entered into the spirit of the event with great enthusiasm.

The Major even managed to find a celebrity to act as an impartial judge and to award prizes. Ralph Whitlock was a well-known broadcaster on BBC radio and had an audience of millions.

Ralph was also a farmer and fully appreciated what it took to raise prize-winning animals and other produce. He was well aware of the limitations of farming on an island and the ingenuity that some of the entrants in the show had had to display in transporting their animals to Tresco from other islands.

On Bryher they had a Jersey cow thought to be the equal of anything in Tresco's herd. They were determined to show the beast, but the problem was: how to get it there?

Islanders are resourceful and practical, particularly the Jenkins family on Bryher.

They had a boat and they had a cow, so they did the logical thing and put the two together to solve the problem.

Fortunately, someone was there with a camera to capture the moment that Bryher's best cow came to the show. The small boy in the picture is Kenny Jenkins,

well-known to visitors and islanders alike as the skipper and part owner of *Firethorn*, the flagship of the islands' boat service.

Today, Kenny – looking more than ever like the *HMS Hero* sailor on the old Players cigarette packet – is retired and still lives on Bryher.

At the Tresco show

By all accounts, these shows were a great success and raised the spirits and morale of islanders at a time of austerity. A great deal of the old 'togetherness' was again re-established as Tresco looked forward to a future that seemed to be cattle and flowers – agricultural rather than tourist.

These photographs open a window on another world. Here is the presentation ceremony presided over by the Major. Radio celebrity Ralph Whitlock has judged the exhibits and will present the prizes. The famous broadcaster addresses the crowd who gather round expectantly. On the blackboard, the name of the Cups and the winners are carefully chalked.

Despite being a time of austerity, everyone made the effort to dress up. Women wore printed summer frocks and hats, men wore jackets and quite often ties and hats. Your clothes in those days were still a statement of status.

Rodney Ward received his prize in tennis clothes. From the blackboard we can see that it was the Cornish Riviera Cup. It also seems to have been a good day for the Major and his wife who between them carried off half of all the prizes. Also listed as a winner is Mrs Ann Oyler, wife of the tenant farmer at Borough Farm in the middle of the island. Today the family still live at the farm.

The Major addresses the islanders. Members of the committee pay close attention

It was a day of bucolic enjoyment; everyone smiling, everyone knowing just where they stood in the community. A good time was had by all. Tresco was back together after the war; a small island at peace with itself.

The Major was held in great affection by the islanders. He was the head of a feudal system that carried responsibilities on all sides. Estate workers laboured hard and loyally for the Estate. In return they could expect a paternalistic concern for their well-being, employment for life and a house for their family until death.

This cradle-to-grave system only worked if there was respect on both sides. It was such an English concept. Other countries had revolutions and could never understand why the English working-man happily accepted a landed class who were so enormously privileged. These pictures show a way of life that was being enacted in villages all over England.

In 1953, the Queen was crowned and Tresco responded with a big party that included the decoration of the island carriage.

Three years later in 1955, the Major died, to the sorrow of all islanders.

His surviving son, Tom, took up the reins.

Tresco celebrates the Queen's Coronation

This picture of the SS Mando *running aground was painted by 'Boy' Lethbridge many years later*

The Seventeenth Chapter

In which the Italian steamer
Mando *gets lost in the fog and
runs aground on Golden Ball Bar*

**The fog on 21 January
1955 was as thick as
anyone could remember.**

**For islanders, the crew of
the Mando – and one
Italian in particular – it
was a day to remember.**

**Lifeboat Coxswain Matt
Lethbridge Senior later
received a Bronze Medal
for the rescue.**

The Mando *at high
water next day*

Matt 'Boy' Lethbridge was on St Mary's and he could hear the steamer blowing loud through the fog.

She had to be very close indeed, he reckoned. After a while, the sound stopped. 'She's either gone away, or she's aground' Matt joked to Jimmy Jenkins, bo'sun of the *Scillonian*.

Within minutes, they knew the truth when Boy's father, Matt Senior found them. Matt Senior, as coxswain of St Mary's lifeboat, had already been alerted by the Coastguard. 'She's aground,' he said, 'Come on....!'

They launched the St Mary's lifeboat at 9 pm at nearly low water. They were forced to take the long passage in the darkness and fog past Samson and White Island, through Castle Bryher Neck, between Gweal and Scilly Rock, then round the top of Bryher.

They believed the *Mando* to be on Men a Vaur because that's what the men at Round Island Light had thought – not being able to see in the fog.

Just before she struck, the *Mando* had erroneously given her position as 87 miles west of the Bishop (probably from her noonday fix). In the fog, she had heard Round Island's foghorn and, believing that she was faced with another vessel dead-ahead, had gone to starboard and run herself onto the unforgiving granite reef that is Golden Ball (or St Helen's) Bar.

Suddenly, through the darkness the lifeboatmen caught sight of the glow of the fire that the *Mando*'s crew had lit on her aft deck.

Abandon ship!

On board the *Mando,* the Italian sailors had lowered their boats, filled them with their possessions and were about to board them from ladders hung from the superstructure.

'Get on board and stop them, or someone's going to get hurt in this swell' Matt Senior told his son.

So 'Boy' leapt aboard, found the Italian captain and persuaded him by sign language to bring his men down to the deck where they could jump into the lifeboat. Matt Senior skillfully kept station in a heavy swell with the engines.

'Boy' helped the captain collect his papers, before they both left the stricken ship – the last to get off.

They took the crew's luggage – already stowed in the *Mando*'s boats – in tow.

They returned through New Grimsby Channel, and while waiting for the tide they transferred the crew's belongings into the lifeboat, leaving the ship's boats to the Bryher men who had put out in a launch.

Suddenly the fog lifted and the lifeboat finally returned to St Mary's at a little after midnight.

Another job well done.

Next day, 'Boy' returned with the Italian captain in a small boat to try to get aboard and retrieve the ship's log, but the *Mando* had already been swamped and the mass of water ebbing and flowing through the scuttles made any return too dangerous.

The sea had claimed her, and she was starting to break up.

Matt 'Boy' Lethbridge photographed at home in St Mary's in 2000

Welcome back!

For one of the seamen rescued from the *Mando* it must have been all too familiar....

On 27 October 1927 – 28 years before – another Italian ship, the *SS Isabo*, struck Scilly Rock in dense fog. In one of the most heroic rescues in Scillonian history 32 of her crew were saved but six perished.

One of the heroes that night was Matt Lethbridge Senior, coxswain of the St Mary's lifeboat.

One crew member that he saved was the young pantry-boy of the *Isabo* who was found clinging to the rigging.

On 21 January 1955 this most unfortunate fellow was once again wrecked in the fog on Scilly in the *Mando* – a mile-and-a-half from his first wreck.

Once again he was rescued by the same lifeboat, under the same coxswain – Matt Lethbridge Senior.

The wreck of the *Mando*

It was a night to remember for Tresco islander John Harding who now lives in Exmouth....

Diamonds or coal dust?

'Although the official record of the wreck of the *Mando* states she was on a voyage from Hampton Roads, USA to Ymuiden in the Netherlands with a cargo of coal dust, it was generally known to all on Scilly that she was actually coming from South Africa to Holland. This being based on her last position and heading.

'I hope so, since many hours were spent on her after she was wrecked looking for smuggled diamonds!

'The fog on 21 January 1955 was the thickest I have encountered. So dense was it, that the sound of the Round Island foghorn could not be heard on Tresco. But the surf of St Helen's Bar could be heard as a constant roar – fog always 'lifts' the height of the groundswell, something I've never been able to fathom out.

'A steamer was 'blowing' to the west of Bryher, the deep sound of a large vessel which echoed through the islands. There was a throatiness about it, a sound of command: "I am here get out of my way". She had been there all afternoon slowly moving NE.'

On short-wave marine radio

'After tea I went to see Ted Eveleigh who was in his greenhouse with Clarence Handy listening to the marine frequency on a short-wave radio.

'We were joined by Bill Gibbons, Sammy Bond, Fred Richards and Frank Naylor – forty years on I still remember the names of all who lived on Tresco, and yet I cannot remember names of work colleagues from five years ago!

'A steamer was talking on Ted's radio. It was the *Mando*. She was loud and clear, so when she gave her position as 280 nautical miles west of Ushant we had our doubts. These doubts must have been shared by Land's End Radio who gave a radio fix.

'As the ship's radio operator was talking we could hear the whistle blow over the radio, and 10-15 seconds later the sound reached us. The steamer had to be the *Mando* and she was less than half a mile from Bolt Head. This information was passed on the phone by Ted Eveleigh to St Mary's Coastguard.

'We were later told that the *Mando* saw Round Island through the fog, heard the foghorn, mistook it for a large vessel, went hard a'starboard and full ahead – straight onto St Helen's Bar.

'The five short blasts on her whistle could be heard throughout the islands. Everyone on Scilly knew that a large steamer was aground to the north.'

Islanders to the rescue

'On St Mary's the lifeboat was launched. On Bryher, brave men put to sea in a gig.

'Today, gigs are in regular use and are seaworthy, but in 1955 the gig *Sussex* that was used that night had not been in the water for years. She must have 'opened up' and leaked like a basket, but launch her they did.

'On St Martin's there was someone with leadership and initiative. They took life-saving equipment, landed on St Helen's and made their way across the island to the Bar; the very area where help would have been needed if the crew had taken to the boats.

'Back on Tresco, Bill Gibbons led the way. He considered taking his boat *The Canadian* to the area where it was thought the *Mando* might be.'

'He asked for volunteers to go with him. Now Bill was a fine boatman; the best, I would have gone anywhere with him – despite the fact that he would make a temporary repair to his Kelvin engine with a piece of string, and a more permanent one with a piece of wire!

'Harry Clement was the first to step forward. Frank Naylor and myself followed. However, we had only a limited knowledge of the area and Bill wanted someone with more experience. So there was a change of plan....

About six of us made our way to Piper's Hole. The fog was thicker than ever – then by a miracle it lifted for a few moments to a height of about 30 feet.

Suddenly we could see flares, search lights and then the port and starboard lights of a large vessel.

Morse Code contact

'Someone produced a powerful torch – my RAF service would come in useful!

'Do you receive me?' I flashed.

The radio officer on *Mando* was quick off the mark.

' "Stop, Stop, Rocks, go to starboard, come astern!" He had mistaken me for another ship.

' "Lifeboat on way, help on way" I flashed. The fog was returning.... "Do you understand?"

' "Yes. Thank you. Thank you."

'With that the fog came down again.

'Someone, Pete Locke I think, ran back to Ted Eveleigh who relayed the above to St Mary's.

'Later the lifeboat reported that all the crew had been taken off and that they had the Bryher gig in tow.

'Then with a laugh: "...and she's full of coal dust!" '

The radio officer on *Mando* was quick off the mark.

'Stop, Stop, Rocks, go to starboard, come astern!'

He had mistaken me for another ship.

The Commander showing the Queen Mother Tresco Abbey Garden on one of her several visits in the 1970s

The Eighteenth Chapter
In which the Commander leads the island into the New Elizabethan Age

Commander Tom Dorrien Smith
1913–1973

Proprietor from 1955

Following the death of his father, Tom Dorrien Smith returned to Tresco to make his home in the Abbey and take over the reins.

Tom retired from the Navy at the end of the war. He married Princess Tamara Imeritinsky. The Imeritinsky family originally came from Georgia, although the Princess had spent her life in Britain.

Georgia's history is steeped in myth and legend. For a thousand years it was ruled by the Bagrationi dynasty. Its Christian knights had withstood the Moslem hordes that swept across Europe – Mongols, Ottomans and Persians.

Georgia eventually splintered as its warring princelings fought each other. The Georgian aristocracy was spread pretty thick; around 6 per cent of the entire population claimed to be nobility. In the first decade of the 19th century the Romanovs, rulers of Russia, annexed various principalities and finally by 1878 the last part of Georgia surrendered. The country then existed only as a region of Russia.

Georgians yearned passionately for independence and revered the memory of their 12th-century Queen Tamara, equivalent to our ancient British Queen Boudicca. Tom's princess bride carried her name of Imeritensky and also that of another Georgian ruling family, the Bagrationis – although it was anglicised to Bagration.

Georgia was also the birthplace of a trainee priest who turned bank-robber – Josef Djugashvili – later better known as the monster Joseph Stalin.

Meanwhile, Tom Dorrien Smith – the Commander – recognised that as the only surviving son he would one day have to run Tresco. He enrolled at agricultural college to study estate management and then purchased a small estate in Somerset.

Once again, it would be time for a change of emphasis if the island was to survive as a private island in the austerity years after the war....

Farming on Tresco in the 1950s

After the war and through the austerity of the 1950s, Tresco relied heavily on the cut-flower industry thanks to the climate advantage it enjoyed over the mainland.

Two farms on the island also produced milk and vegetables.

The Commander inherited a Garden that was attracting 17,000 paying visitors a year. However, it did not generate enough revenue to sustain the team of gardeners and the attendant maintenance costs.

Elsewhere on the island was a substantial stock of cottages and farm buildings that could be used as holiday accommodation.

The Commander made a decision; he would share his lovely island with visitors who would pay to holiday there....

Tresco's cut-flower industry

Bunching and packing of the narcissi was a well-regulated production line.

There was even a 'flower railway' making use of the unused rails and bogeys left over from the First World War Naval Air Station.

The system could be taken up and relaid very easily, rather like a large toy train set. It was used extensively in the trenches in northern France and elsewhere to transport supplies to the front line.

This delightful picture of a proud island mother in Old Grimsby was taken by an unknown visiting press photographer.

The mother is Gloria Lawry with her two daughters.

Gloria is now a pensioner on Tresco.

1960 – The Island Hotel opens

Three years after Tom inherited Tresco, he selected a small number of cottages to be used for holiday letting during the summer. They were simple island cottages with basic facilities, but they proved extremely popular.

Two years after that, the Commander felt confident enough to convert and enlarge some old coastguard cottages in Old Grimsby into the Island Hotel. It opened for business in 1960.

The Queen Mother on Tresco in the 1960s and 1970s

The New Elizabethan Age

>## Devoted to his island home

The Commander's decision meant that Tresco had taken its first steps towards becoming a tourist destination for a limited number of people. In doing so he secured the future of the island community and – of course – the Abbey Garden.

Princess Tamara Imeritinsky bore him five children: Teona, Alexandra, Robert, Charlotte and James. The family were expected to take a close interest in the Garden and all took part in the practical work of maintaining it.

The Commander was elected as Chairman of the Isles of Scilly Council – unlike his forbears who inherited the office by right of birth. The family continued to exert considerable, and democratic, influence over all the islands.

Under his leadership, the Tresco Abbey Garden continued to expand as new species were introduced.

In 1963 the Commander took his mother Eleanor on a trip retracing her 1910 honeymoon trip to Western Australia and New Zealand. They returned with a mass of rare plants collected from the major botanic gardens on the eastern Australian coast with which to enrich the Abbey Garden. The Commander also built contact with botanical gardens all over the world.

The Commander enjoyed telling the Tresco story with enthusiasm and vivid descriptions – whether he was lecturing the Royal Horticultural Society or talking to friends. He lived a life committed to Tresco, and always took a leading part in island activities.

The Commander was divorced from Tamara in 1967 and married Peggy Worthington, a widow, with whom he enjoyed seven happy years until his death in 1973.

The Queen Mother was an enthusiastic and knowledgeable gardener and visited Tresco many times in the 1960s and 1970s during the Commander's tenure as Proprietor. On one occasion she arranged for a gift of a flock of canaries that she thought would thrive among the sub-tropical vegetation. Unfortunately they were all blown out to sea in a winter gale and none survived.

May Day in the 1950s

Islander Eddie Birch, above as a young child and, right, nearest the camera, on a May Day in the 1950s

Eddie Birch remembers May Day in the 1950s....

'We had the donkey cart all decorated up. The May Queen was crowned on the School Green, and then we'd have a procession up to the Abbey.

'The babies would sit in the donkey cart with the great iron wheels, and the mothers followed behind. We'd sing some songs up there and then go to every house, sing a song, take a few handfuls of gorse petals that the mothers had collected from the Downs and sprinkle them for luck on the doorstep. Then down to the Farm for lunch, and carry on round the island.

'The eldest boy always led the procession, carrying a Union Jack. I was once the eldest boy when my sister Jean was the May Queen. It was all just a good bit of fun to us.'

Fun during the austerity years

Fetes and Fancy-dress

The whole island community turned out for fetes and enjoyed themselves, as these snapshots show.

Rationing was still in force – the Tresco tomato stand has the sales pitch ' No Coupon'.

An island wedding

Ned Steele the Cobbler

Ned Steele, the one-legged cobbler, was an island character. Jean Elliot (nee Harding), who now lives in Kelso, Scotland, remembers Ned and his wife Emma well:

'As a teenager in the early 50s I lodged with Emma and Ned Steele when I worked in the Estate Office.

'Emma had a budgie which was partial to a drop of beer when Ned came home from an evening at the New Inn. The budgie was poorly and Emma prepared a shoe box lined with moss for a burial. However, she was advised to give the budgie some grass, so the box was put back in the shed and the budgie survived to entertain us for a while longer.

'One day a neighbour asked if Emma and Ned had cast out. "No," said I (thinking, nosey beggar!). "Well", he said "when they are talking, his pyjamas and her nightdress hang together on the line. If they had cast out they hung at each end of the line!".

Glenys Mackie (nee Venn, now living in Powys, Wales was a child on Tresco in the 50s. She never forgot Ned:

'I remember Ned working in his cobbler's shop and sticking the huge leather-needles into his wooden leg. As a little girl, when I tried this on my own leg with a darning needle, my father explained that cobblers had wooden legs especially to hold their needles!'

Royal Visits

The Queen and Prince Philip visited Tresco, bringing a young Prince Charles and Princess Anne with them. For Prince Charles it was an opportunity to look around the islands that would eventually be part of his responsibility as Duke of Cornwall.

The Royal party were hosted by The Commander, his wife and two daughters.

Football teams in the 1950s

Sport was taken extremely seriously on the island, and there were enough fit men for Old Grimsby and New Grimsby to have a team each.

Rivalry was intense and to be made Captain of the Cricket Club or Football Club was considered to be a prime achievement and carried with it considerable social kudos.

It was, in many ways, rather like being at school.

Tresco Abbey

> ## The Nineteenth Chapter
> *In which young Robert Dorrien Smith inherits an island in dire financial straits*

Robert A Dorrien Smith
1951–

Proprietor from 1973

Following the death of the Commander in 1973, Robert Dorrien Smith inherited the Estate at the age of 22.

As the last quarter of the 20th century approached, Tresco's small community appeared to be a successful example of Benthamism. However, it had been at a cost and most of it had fallen on the Dorrien Smiths.

Robert was only 22 when his father died. A year later Harold Wilson's second Labour government was elected with a promise to squeeze the rich 'until the pips sqeaked'. Owners of estates like Tresco were now squarely in the cross-hairs of their socialist rulers.

Robert had not just inherited an island, he had also inherited a mountain of debt. Only a creative solution could possibly save the way of life that islanders enjoyed.

The scheme that became the solution involved a new way of using the island's holiday cottages. It was based on a concept that had been successful in Swiss ski resorts.

The idea was to offer visitors a 40-year lease on just the slice of time that they wanted to use in a holiday cottage – rather than offering them the whole property. Several families could now share a holiday cottage, actually owning their time in it. It was affordable, and quickly proved very popular. The first timeshare cottages on Tresco were occupied in 1978. Essential capital for the Estate had been raised without losing control of the property, visitors were guaranteed their holiday reservation each year and the island was certain of fully occupied cottages.

It was an elegant solution.

Mr Robert takes charge

'Tresco Children' by David Wynne

Still in his twenties 'Mr Robert', as he was known to islanders, was now in charge of an island community that looked to him for leadership and for their future security.

Private islands get few grants, and Tresco had quickly to become financially self-sufficient.

Gradually the team was built and standards raised. The Island Hotel that the Commander had created was extended and more cottages were converted to holiday letting.

Environmental projects also benefited; the reeds were cleared around the Great Pool to create a wetland for migratory birds; a sewage system was installed so that the waters around Tresco always remained clear and unpolluted.

In 1987 the old engine house was closed. No longer would the island generate its own electricity – Tresco was connected to the national grid. Suddenly unheard-of luxuries such as washing machines and dishwashers could be used.

The island was back on its feet; for the benefit of both islanders and visitors alike. In 1983 a direct helicopter link was opened between Penzance and Tresco.

The Queen Mother was an enthusiastic gardener and always enjoyed her visits to the Abbey Garden – this one in June 1985.

She also enjoyed her first ride on one of Tresco's tractor-drawn 'buses'.

With Robert Dorrien Smith and bearded Head Gardener Mike Nelhams

At the Valhalla figurehead museum

Art in the Garden

The Abbey Garden was savaged by a snow storm in 1987 and then by a hurricane in 1990. Once again the gardeners were called on to restore and replant.

The result was magnificent. They looked on the positive side and found new areas of sheltered sunshine in which to plant, while gradually replacing the damaged shelter-belt.

Together, Robert and Lucy Dorrien Smith started to create a private art collection by West Country artists who have been inspired by the island. Gallery Tresco was created out of an old gig shed to encourage and promote local artists, craftsmen and women.

Two fine sculptures by David Wynne were positioned in the Abbey Garden. *Tresco Children,* modelled on Robert's three older children, is positioned at the lower end of the Garden at the end of an important vista.

Gaia is modelled on David Wynne's wife Gill. The beautifully striated South African marble block from which it is shaped was considered too difficult to be carved. Beatle George Harrison bought it and gave it to David Wynne as a challenge. He was right to do so. David Wynne eventually created a masterpiece.

Riding the Tresco 'bus'

The Prince and Princess of Wales visited St Mary's and Tresco in 1982 when the Princess was expecting their first child – William

*Robert Dorrien Smith and
the Princess of Wales*

The Dorrien Smiths and the Duchy

When Augustus Smith came to Scilly in 1834 he lifted the island communities out of poverty and encouraged enlightened self-interest among the islanders. Those who wanted to help themselves were given the means and encouragement to do so. This had not been understood or appreciated by his peers on the mainland. But he stood alone, and he prospered.

His descendants Thomas, Arthur, Tom and Robert have each built on the foundations laid by Augustus. Each inherited problems, saw opportunities, found solutions and each time the island community benefited.

The Dorrien Smiths held the lease, first of the whole of the Isles of Scilly, and later of Tresco. Their landlord was, and is, the Duchy of Cornwall.

The Duchy is a private estate that funds the public, charitable and private activities of the Prince of Wales and his family. Today, it consists of around 54,648 hectares of land in 23 counties, mostly in the south west of England.

The Duchy estate was created in 1337 by Edward III for his son and heir, Prince Edward the Black Prince, and its primary function was to provide him and future Princes of Wales with an income from its assets. A charter ruled that each future Duke of Cornwall would be the eldest surviving son of the Monarch and the heir to the throne.

Relationships between landlord and tenant can often be sensitive, and from an outsider's view it looks like the Duchy and the Smiths often existed in a state of armed neutrality. In fact, Augustus Smith felt strongly enough to make sure that after his death he would be buried at St Buryan on the Cornish mainland rather than rest in Duchy land.

His descendants continued the work of maintaining a community that could support itself financially. Their various improvements and investments have made Tresco what it is today. Occasionally disagreements with their landlord became an issue and had to resolved more or less amicably. However, there has always been a generous and loyal welcome for every Prince of Wales who has visited Tresco over the years.

In 1992, ten years after their first visit, the Prince and Princess of Wales holidayed on Tresco with Princes William and Harry. It would be their last family holiday together.

A Feudal Society

Robert and Lucy Dorrien Smith

A week after these photographs were taken, Andrew Morton's book *Diana: Her True Story* was published and personal problems became very public ones.

Today, Tresco is still a paternalistic community and one in which islanders are encouraged to show initiative and enterprise. The Proprietor is benevolent and employees are fiercely loyal.

It may be an old-fashioned society, out of fashion even, but it could be the best sort of society there is. Certainly thousands of visitors are attracted every year to relish for a while a quality of life that can no longer be found on the mainland.

This kind of feudal society also throws up an anomaly: on Tresco one man owns everything. This means that no one else owns anything. However, what looks like great inequality actually creates a society of equals. No one owns their own house, no one has a car, no one dresses up or wears a collar and tie.

Materialism, together with the envy that runs with it, is therefore absent. In a funny way, it's the sort of Utopia that followers of Communism thought they could achieve. Maybe Augustus Smith and Jeremy Bentham are sitting on a cloud and quietly nodding approval that an experiment started nearly two centuries ago has flourished.

For the Dorrien Smith family, Tresco continues to be their home, to provide employment for the island community and a relaxed holiday for visitors.

The next generation is represented by Adam, Frances and Michael from Robert's first marriage to Lady Emma Windsor Clive, and by Marina and Tristan from his marriage to Lucy Morgan Smith.

The starboard sponson broke off in the crash and was found floating at the scene. It is being loaded onto the Scillonian

The Twentieth Chapter
In which fog once again takes a deadly toll in the summer of 1983

On 26 April 1983 Robert Dorrien Smith and Sir John King, Chairman of British Airways, opened Tresco heliport. Oscar November *crashed three months later. Sister aircraft* Delta Alpha *is in the background in this official photograph.*

On Saturday 16 July 1983, at the start of the school summer holidays, a British Airways Sikorsky S-61, with 23 passengers and a crew of three lifted off from Penzance bound for St Mary's and Tresco.

Oscar November (G-BEON) left on-time at 12.40 and was scheduled to arrive on St Mary's 20 minutes later. She crashed over the sea two-and-a-half miles short of St Mary's.

Twenty people died.

Take-off from Penzance

O*scar November* normally operated in the North Sea. She was based in Aberdeen and flew a shuttle service to the oil-rigs.

On 22 June 1983 she underwent her annual certificate of airworthiness. Two days later she was transferred to Penzance to operate to the Isles of Scilly as a replacement for the usual helicopter that had been running the service since it had been bought new in 1974. That helicopter had been taken out of service for repairs and a full overhaul.

It was foggy that day, but conditions were within British Airway's minimum weather regulations of 900 metres visibility that permit the pilot to fly on visual alone. Pilot Dominic Lawlor and co-pilot Neil Charleton therefore decided to take off.

Interestingly, the pilots' union BALPA had recommended that 900 metres be increased to one nautical mile following the crash of a

Bell 212 in bad visibility in the North Sea two years before. Had these proposals been accepted the pilots would been compelled to fly using both instruments and visual.

The 23 passengers were almost entirely holiday-makers, although there were two Scillonians on board – Mrs Lucille Langley-Williams and Mrs Megan Smith.

The passengers boarded, families seating themselves in the pairs of forward-facing seats, leaving the single seats to be occupied by Mrs Langley-Williams, Mrs Smith and two children who sat across the aisle from their parents.

Over the roar of the engines, they listened to the on-board safety brief, then the flight attendant checked that they were all strapped-in. *Oscar November* lifted off and started her flight to Scilly....

Through the fog and into a fog-bank

In the cockpit, pilot Dominic Lawlor was flying at 250 feet over the sea and beneath the worst of the fog. He was flying on visual and instruments and was still within the airline's weather regulations to be doing so. Down below, he could see the sea – pretty much flat calm.

If you talk to Navy helicopter pilots who are trained to land helicopters on the stern of frigates at night in very poor visibility they will tell you that it is extremely hard to repress all information they receive from their eyes and ears and to subordinate it to the information from their instruments. It's unnatural, and takes a lot of training before they learn completely not to trust their senses.

Two-and-a-half miles from St Mary's and beginning to line up on an approach, *Oscar November* ran into a thick fog-bank. There was no way to fly under it. Pilot Lawlor switched from visual and instruments to visual only. He would rely on his eye-sight.

Lawlor peered through the windscreen desperately trying to keep the sea below him in view. His glimpses of it came and went in the fog. He maintained height by feel and instinct, all the time looking down to catch sight of the sea.

By this time they were in regular radio contact with St Mary's tower.

At 12.58 – 18 minutes after take-off from Penzance – St Mary's tower lost all contact with *Oscar November*.

No Mayday call had been received.

A few minutes later, St Mary's guessed the worst and actioned the emergency procedure. The maroons went up for the launch of St Mary's lifeboat, and the Royal Navy at Culdrose scrambled the Search and Rescue helicopters.

Impact

At 12.57 pilot Lawlor was guiding *Oscar November* through the fog-bank and was now down below 250 feet. Desperately trying to catch a glimpse of the sea, he was hindered by constantly having to glance at the altimeter that was inconveniently positioned by his knee. He was now becoming completely disorientated.

At 12.58 *Oscar November* hit the sea at speed, bouncing several times before coming to rest.

It was a violent impact. The helicopter's nose cone was torn off, as were the sponsons – the wheel housing and flotation pods on each side of the fuselage. Three of the five main rotor blades sheared off, as did the tail rotor. The fuselage was badly damaged amd the floor was opened up as if by a tin-opener.

Within a couple of seconds the roar of the engines were silenced and the helicopter became eight tons of metal with a gaping hole in it. It started to sink like a stone.

In the cabin, the impact had tragic consequences. All of the twin seats were ripped from their mountings and collapsed onto each other trapping the occupants. Only the single seats remained fixed.

Lucille Langley-Williams, Megan Smith and the two children in the single seats were the only survivors from the cabin. The children were orphaned.

Mrs Langley-Williams told *The Times*'s reporter 'It was very quick. I bumped forwards and hit my head on the seat in front.' She asked her friend Mrs Smith 'What the hell is going on?' The response was one word before the passengers were all chest-deep in seawater.

Her seat had twisted on impact and tightened the belt. 'I closed my mouth and took a deep breath and by then I was under water. I realised I had not got an awful lot of breath left.' She released the belt, somehow opened the door and floated upwards.

On the surface she found five other survivors: the two children, both pilots and her friend Mrs Smith. None of them had had time to don life-jackets. They heard the maroons go off on St Mary's and knew the lifeboat would be looking for them.

Rescue

On St Mary's, coxswain Matt 'Boy' Lethbridge took out the lifeboat *Robert Edgar* and set off into the fog. Even in the summer, the Atlantic is cold and he knew he did not have much time if anyone was to survive in the water.

It must have been like trying to find a needle in a haystack, but somehow – through skill, intuition or plain luck – Matt found them. They were cold and shocked, but alive.

Meanwhile the helicopters from RNAS Culdrose were helpless, unable to see anything through the fog.

Mrs Langley-Williams said 'It was the most wonderful moment in my life to see the coxswain's face as he reached down over the side of the lifeboat.'

Lifeboat coxswain Matt Lethbridge helps a survivor up the steps at St Mary's

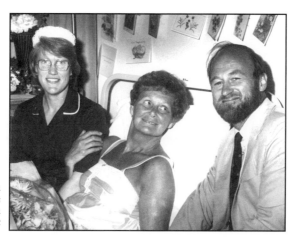

Lucille Langley-Smith recovering in St Mary's hospital, with Dr Adrian Davies and Sister Irene Hunt

Recovery

The fuselage of Oscar November is visible on the stern of RMAS Seaforth Clansman *after recovery*

On 19 July, three days after the accident, *Oscar November* was recovered from 200 feet down by *RMAS Seaforth Clansman*. She was attended by the Penlee lifeboat *Mabel Alice*. The wreck was located by her Cator beacon Seventeen bodies were recovered. Most of the passengers still had their seat-belts fastened.

Initially there was speculation that a bird-strike might have been responsible as a number of seagull corpses had been seen in the vicinity of the crash by those first on the scene. However, similar corpses were found at other places on Scilly. On inspection, the grille that prevents birds from entering the engines was found to be intact and undamaged, so the bird-strike theory was dismissed.

Oscar November was transported to the Government's air accident investigation branch – the Royal Aircraft Establishment at Farnborough.

The accident investigation report was published 20 months later in February 1985. It concluded that the pilot Dominic Lawlor, although flying within British Airways regulations, had become disorientated in the fog and descended into the sea without realising that he was doing so.

The cause of the accident was officially 'pilot error'.

The report also made eight important recommendations.

Recommendations and safety issues

The main recommendations were that all passenger helicopters be fitted with an audible height warning, and that the altimeter be moved into the pilot's head-up line of vision.

The report also proposed that the strength of passenger seats should be improved. It recommended a review of minimum visibility standards, as had been suggested by the pilots' union. Pilots should also wear lifejackets with personal beacons and improvements should be made in barometric pressure indicators. The full report remains protected and embargoed in the National Archives until after 1 January 2016.

Prior to the report, and a few days after the accident, *The Times* reported that one of their freelance journalists had flown on *Oscar November* four days prior to the accident. In an interview with British Airways directors, after the accident, she raised several points.

Her passenger ticket was anonymous, simply marked 'Body'. The onboard safety demonstration was inaudible over the engine noise. There were no safety cards in the seat-back. No attention was drawn to the emergency exits and baggage was left in the aisle and in front of the exits.

On 25 March 1985 in the House of Commons, and in response to a question from local MP David Harris, Michael Spicer speaking for the Government said that seven of the eight recommendations had been accepted by the Civil Aviation Authority.

The only one not accepted was the use of aerodrome pressure settings on low-level approaches to St Mary's.

Today, passengers can relax knowing that in the 25 years since the accident a far more rigorous safety regime has been instituted, and that everyone has learnt from the terrible events of 16 July 1983.

A last sad postcript

For one family – all of whom died in the accident – there was a final cruelty. Both parents died intestate – with no will.

English law assumes that in accidents such as this one, that individuals die in order of age. As a result, the father was deemed to have died first, his estate then being taxed before passing to his wife.

Her estate was taxed before passing to the children whose estates were then taxed in turn.

Penzance solicitor David James was retained by relatives to examine all the forensic evidence to see if it could be proved that the father or mother had possibly survived a few minutes longer than their children.

It was a deeply distressing task that he has never forgotten – particularly as he was ultimately unsuccessful.

An island funeral

The Twenty-First Chapter
*In which an islander leaves
Tresco on her final journey*

She was elderly, in her late seventies, and she died quite suddenly on a bright spring afternoon. The last thing she would have seen was the sunlit harbour, and the last thing she would have heard was the sound of the birds and the mewing of the seagulls.

The scent of cut grass was in her nostrils since they had cut the verges that very afternoon. For her it was not such a bad death.

For her family left behind it was hard, and the community knew that; their concern was for her children and grandchildren and it was demonstrated in small acts of kindness. No one was maudlin or sentimental. They were sad because she had been well-liked, loved even. On Tresco the veil between life and death is thin.

So life went on much the same as usual for the rest of the week.

The funeral was at 2 o'clock in the church of St Nicholas that sits at the bottom of the hill in Dolphin Town. It has a quiet and loving atmosphere. Like many places where good people congregate, it has absorbed beautiful thoughts and prayers in its stones and gives them back to anyone sensitive enough to receive them. It is a place deeply cared for, and it is well looked after by the community. It has a purpose.

An island funeral

As islanders gathered before the service, chatting quietly in the graveyard, the sun came out. Everyone had changed into their Sunday best, the men in suits and jackets that had not been worn since the last funeral or wedding, running a finger round a shirt collar too tight against the neck. The women, also in black, were much more put-together. Somehow, every woman seems to have a dark outfit that fits her.

Everyone takes their place in the church. Suddenly, we are awkward, eyes averted. The time is coming to say goodbye. The coffin, covered in flowers, stands before the choir.

We sit, each immersed in contemplation of mortality. Robert and Lucy Dorrien Smith take their places in the family pew. Six men of the island sit next to them in dark suits. They are pall-bearers. They look nervous.

It is a mixed congregation. Honest faces, tanned or weathered – from all the islands. The youngsters blooming in health. Older ones moving slowly. Some latecomers arrive, straight from their jobs and still in work-clothes. The undertaker shows them to the last seats in the congregation.

> *Was there ever such a dignified undertaker? With white hair and beard he looks like God.*

Then he returns, leading the family to their pews in the front. Was there ever such a dignified undertaker? With white hair and beard he looks like God. Nothing escapes him, his care and solicitude for the bereaved, his whole body language – everything about him encapsulates why we are here.

Finally, all are seated and our vicar Donald Marr starts the service. He knows each of us well. He will bind us together, express our feelings, focus our sympathy for the bereaved. He starts by reminding us of the beauty of our surroundings, outside and in. He tells us that we are here to celebrate a life....

It is a simple service, and it is right. We sing the hymns that she loved and which we all know. Emotion starts to be released ... *How Great Thou Art*! Tresco's Headmaster reads the lesson. Then prayers, resonating with the poetry of ritual, full of comfort.

Then we are singing again. *Bread of Heaven*! Donald speaks from the pulpit. His words are well chosen. We all knew her well; there is no need to express anything but the simple love and affection that we all hold. It is well done.

A long moment of silent contemplation, more prayers and then the final hymn. Donald advances to the coffin, blesses her. There is a deep, deep tension. This is goodbye.

The undertaker returns. A nod of his head, and the pall-bearers take up their places. Their wooden carrying bars slide into the strops. They take the strain, the undertaker removes the trestles under the coffin, and slowly – ever so slowly and carefully – the pall-bearers turn until they face the congregation.

The organ plays *The Old Rugged Cross* as Donald and the undertaker lead the way. Behind them, with down-cast eyes, the pall-bearers walk the coffin still covered in flowers, through the congregation to the door at the back of the church. The island is saying goodbye and many are in tears.

The family leave the church, and we follow. Outside, she is lowered gently into the warm earth of Tresco to lie next to others who went before her. Handfuls of earth are tossed into the grave. Donald speaks the final words of comfort and commitment. We watch from a distance as the family say their last farewells.

Standing outside the church in the sunshine, friends from other islands – not seen for a while – greet each other. Conversation starts. Quiet, still reverent.

Soon we walk to the Hotel behind the family. Under a canopy, drinks and sandwiches are served. The family circulate, talking to friends, shaking hands, hugging. There's relief in the air. The island has said goodbye. Laughter is heard again.

For those that are left, life must go on – and that is as it should be....

> *For those that are left, life must go on – and that is as it should be....*

On the left of the picture is Greenside – my home with Kathy for 14 years.
It is now a holiday cottage

<table>
<tr><td>

The Twenty-Second Chapter
In which I start work – and the Tresco Times *becomes a quarterly magazine*

</td></tr>
</table>

I started work in the Tresco Estate Office in October 1991. My task was to fill the island's holiday cottages with holidaymakers.

But with no passing-trade, how would we get the message out?

The first edition of the Tresco Times *was produced by Wendy Gleadle*

That first day on Tresco when Kathy and I arrived on the island, we had walked up into the wild and ancient North End of Tresco where we fell asleep in the sun, lying on heather and listening to the sound of the waves. Around us were the shades of Bronze Age man in a vast prehistoric burial ground. It was as magical a place as anyone could imagine.

Something entered our soul and we were touched by a sense of history and the achingly beautiful natural world around us – beaches, cliffs, clear blue sea, plants and birdlife. This sensual awakening stirred our creativity.

Kathy is an artist and to this day Tresco remains an inspiration. Her oils and prints capture the

beauty and, above all, the tranquillity and spirit of the island in a very gentle and feminine way. She wants other people to be touched by it as we were. Her work does that for the many who hang her pictures in their homes.

My background was more prosaic. I was a copywriter and marketing man who painted his pictures with words. My job was to find a way to bring the magic of Tresco to an audience who might want to holiday on the island. This magic could not be conveyed simply by photos of beaches and palm trees, it was an abstract thing – best conjured with words rather than images. Words can be worth a thousand pictures.

It happened that a colleague in the Estate Office, Wendy Gleadle had just produced a corporate newsletter for the island – the *Tresco Times*. Perhaps this could be the vehicle to spread the magic....

Good News on Sewage!

The first edition of the *Tresco Times* was intended as a newsletter that would update regular visitors on any improvements and changes to the island. The first editor, Wendy Gleadle, wrote it under the direction of Robert Dorrien Smith. It was then passed to the design department of the printer. The result was a somewhat municipal effort. The events that excited the editor – worthy stuff about sewage, sea defences and woodland maintenance – seemed unlikely to make readers exclaim 'Brilliant, we must book a holiday there'.

But what would persuade readers to take a holiday on the island?

The first essential was to acquire a computer. Incredible though it may seem today, in 1991 there was only one computer on the island and that belonged to the Accounts Department who were therefore also the IT department.

Fortunately, we acquired a computer for the *Tresco Times* although the only programme on it was a very basic word-processing one. Flashy programmes like Word from the fledgling Microsoft company were out of the question, and the idea of a Mac – well, forget it.

Wendy very generously let me take over as editor, and we produced the first desk-top published *Tresco Times*. It could hardly have been more basic: one sheet of folded A3 proudly inscribed 'Issue No. 2'. We photocopied it ourselves and distributed it on the island and by post to our timeshare owners.

It contained published timeshare prices and other information plus some jokes. Not very good ones, but it was the start of a slightly tongue-in-cheek attitude – *'The Island Hotel manager, Ivan Curtis, has asked us to mention that there is a dress code in the restaurant in the evening – jackets and ties should be worn. Other clothing is presumably optional'.*

Up to that point, when someone wrote to the Estate Office for a brochure no record was kept. The brochure was sent and their letter was binned. Now that we had a computer their name and address was entered and we had the beginnings of what was to become the *Tresco Times* subscriber list.

What to write about?

Although we emphasised the beauty of the island and the quality of the accommodation, it quickly became apparent that what made Tresco unique was the small island community of around 130 residents. Visitors wanted to feel part of island life when they were on holiday. Many who had been coming for years had formed close friendships with island residents.

Right from the beginning, we wrote about the small successes and the occasional sadnesses of the people who lived on Tresco. It proved to be exactly what the readers wanted.

Soon the *Tresco Times* was being published quarterly, and within a couple of years the subscriber list had grown to 4,000 – almost all of which were posted free to subscribers at home.

Some readers who wrote for a brochure found that they could not afford Tresco's prices, but the *Tresco Times* kept coming to remind them that perhaps one day they could come for a holiday here. For a great many this worked, and they came to visit Tresco later – when they could afford it.

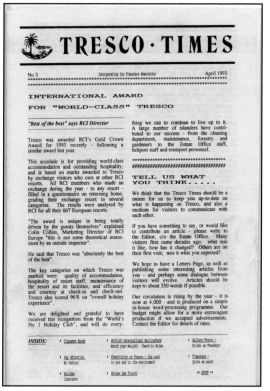

An early copy produced with a primitive word-processing and expanded to 8 pages of A4

Island faces

Layouts and Strap-lines

By the end of 1993, two years after we took the *Tresco Times* fully in-house, we finally were given the Microsoft Word programme. This allowed a slightly more professional-looking newsletter, although we were not able to include either colour or photographs.

This did not seem a great problem at the time as we still wanted to get the message over in words rather than pictures. Words are better at conveying atmosphere, humour and set the tone of voice with which we wanted to speak to the readership.

We also adopted the first of several strap lines – *'Our Views are Clear'* had a good double meaning. We later added the punning *'Making Sense of Scilly'* and *'About the Last Piece of England'* – another double meaning.

The subscriber list was growing, doubling every year, and the amount of holidays being sold that could be attributed directly to the *Tresco Times* was growing in parallel.

It was time to take the paper to the next level....

A 1994 issue, produced entirely in the Microsoft Word programme

Colour photos..... and The Commodore

In order to be able to continue to both write and to lay out the *Tresco Times* I needed to be trained as a layout artist, and so took a three-day course in London. After that I would be learning on the job.

The first few full-colour editions were a bit shaky, but soon things began to look pretty good – quirky, but good. I bought a high-quality camera to take the photographs.

Our new full colour edition introduced the Commodore and his page called *'A Waffle with the Commodore'*. He has been a regular contributor ever since and his forthright plain-speaking has earned him many fans and a few left-wing enemies.

Seventeen years after the first issue of the *Tresco Times* the paper has a print-run of 45,000 and is posted out free around the world. The most important subject continues to be the story of the 130 islanders who make up the permanent population.

A full-colour issue from 1999, covering the Eclipse

One book ends, and another begins...

Still going strong.... for the moment

Goodness knows how long the *Tresco Times* will continue, but up until now it has been enormous fun to write and it has justified its existence by bringing thousands of vistors to Tresco over the years.

Sitting here today, 17 years after first becoming editor, I look back with a quiet chuckle.

The Isles of Scilly Council once ordered all copies of the *Tresco Times* on St Mary's to be burned in the council incinerator, Government ministers quoted us in Parliament, our stories have been recycled in the *The Times*, *The Sunday Times*, *The Independent*, *The Telegraph* and by Danny Baker on Radio London. Our Tresco cricket reports have beeen debated on 'Test Match Special'.

We were the second paper in the UK to publish on the internet, behind *The Daily Telegraph* but ahead of Murdoch's *Times*.

Our beady eye has been kept on a series of politicians on both sides of the Atlantic....

At least two people read every copy of the *Tresco Times* – that's 90,000 readers for each issue. This is the number of people that fit into Wembley Stadium for a Cup Final. The population of Tresco could all stand comfortably within the centre circle.

Above all, the *Tresco Times* is about the people of Tresco who have made it unique.

They are the community of which you become part – even if only for a short time.

So, one book ends and another begins....

This volume has covered some of the stories of Tresco from the Bronze Age up to the present.

The next volume – *'Our Views are Clear'* – contains full pages and extracts from the *Tresco Times* and describes in full colour the stories and lives of modern Tresco islanders.

ACKNOWLEDGEMENTS

The first edition of *The Last Piece of England* was published by Halsgrove in 2002. The book was set out by Halsgrove in their standard format for regional histories. At a pre-publication meeting I protested that a different design was called for. Simon Butler, the Managing Director and my editor, disagreed. The debate ended with Simon saying 'Richard, how many books have you published?' 'None' I replied. 'I have published hundreds' said Simon 'so I think we'll do it my way'.

The result was a book that sold out very quickly, so I have to admit that Simon had a point.

However, I still longed for my vision of *The Last Piece of England* to become tangible and, with a generosity for which I am eternally grateful, Simon released the copyright so that I could lay it out and publish it myself in two extended volumes.

This is Volume One, and I hope that it will be at least as successful as the Halsgrove edition. I owe a big thank-you to Simon and to Halsgrove.

Every book needs a good cover, by which it should, of course, never be judged. One of my closest friends, Denis Cairnes, designed it in return for some decent claret. Denis is now nearer eighty than seventy so I am grateful that he agreed to come temporarily out of retirement to provide another example of his graphic art.

Fiona Holman generously proof-read the manuscript for me, and devoted a great deal of care and time to it. I could not have published it without her friendly help. I am immensely grateful.

The surviving members of the Special Forces who operated from Tresco, and their families, entrusted me with carefully written, unpublished memoirs. I hope I have done these heroes justice. Sir Brooks Richards helped arrange the reunion on Tresco, and allowed me to quote from his book *Secret Flotillas*.

This book is largely about the Dorrien Smiths, and Robert and Lucy Dorrien Smith kindly gave me free access to their family photgraph albums. Helen Dorrien Smith corrected me on several points of detail about the family. Sandra Gibson-Klyne provided a mass of photographs from the wonderful Gibson Collection archive on Scilly. Maritime archivist Raymond Forward supplied the *Isabo* photographs.